MIRACLES
DO HAPPEN

A B-17 Navigator's Story of the September 11, 1944

Mission to Destroy the Ruhland, Germany Oil Refinery

and His Prison Camp Experience In Stalag Luft I

by Donald H. Lienemann

Donald H. Lienemann

Navigator 1st Lt 1104 Base ...

Cover and book design by Julie Fahrlander
Photographer Brett Hampton

Library of Congress Cataloging-in-Publication Data

Lienemann, Donald H.
  Miracles do happen : a B-17 navigator's story of the September 11, 1944 mission to destroy the Ruhland, Germany oil refinery and his prison camp experience in Stalag Luft I / by Donald H. Lienemann ; cover by Julie Fahrlander
     p. cm.
     ISBN 0-9747525-0-9

     1.   Lienemann, Donald H. 2. World War, 1939-1945--Personal narratives, American. 3. United States. Army Air Forces. Air Force, 8th-Biography. 4. World War, 1939-1945-Aerial operations, American. 5. World War, 1939-1945-Campaigns-Germany. 6. Stalag Luft I. 7. Prisoners of war-United States-Biography. 8. Prisoners of war-Germany-Biography. I. Title.

D811.L455 2003   940.54'213'092
                            QBI03-200917

Printed in the USA
By Morris Publishing
3212 E. Hwy 30
Kearney, NE 68847

Dedication

This book is gratefully dedicated to those parents, wives, brothers and sisters of the six gallant men on my crew who met such an untimely, yet heroic death on the raid over Ruhland, Germany, September 11, 1944. To all of them, also to the untold thousands of other families, who have suffered a similar loss, goes my heartfelt sympathy and understanding.

You have made the supreme sacrifice, and have given all, yea even life itself, and may I be the first to compliment you on the spirit with which you have carried on your work under such a burden. May the patriotism you have shown and the sacrifice you made-be not in vain, but rather a guiding light to the millions of other Americans who gave so little by comparison. These boys died so this, the America that we live in, might be a better country in which to pursue freedom and happiness. Let us therefore all carry on so that they shall not have died in vain, and may they in turn rest in peace, knowing full well that we will do our utmost to make this the better country for which they died.

My heartfelt thanks to my loving Aunt, Christine S. Marth, for attending my graduation from navigation school at Ellington Field in Houston, and for her assistance in typing the original copy of this manuscript.

Prison camp diary entries in memory of the crew memers who died.

by Donald H. Lienemann

MIRACLES DO HAPPEN

Table of Contents

Chapter I
Preparation and Briefing

Sure enough, there comes the jeep down the hill now, and it can mean but one thing. In a few minutes I shall know the answer. O yes, it buzzed on around the block first, for that is the only way that it can make its way up into the W.A.A.F. site, which is where we are billeted. (The Lucky Shack, Hut 17, given this name because not a man has ever been lost from it, but oh what a change is going to be made in the records in the next 24 hours!) Little did I dream or even think of that as the C.Q. walked in the door and asked for Baker's crew, of which I was the navigator. I had been waiting for him and greeted him as he entered for I knew when the jeep approached and came to a screeching halt that it had to be us. The other crew had just gone on Flak Leave, so it could be no one else. It was early... much earlier than most people back in the States ever once suspected, 01:15 A.M. to be exact. At this time only the bombardier, Lt. McGuinness and I had to get up, for we were to go to the lead crew briefing, and study the target for the day. Before arising however we did ask him what the gas load for the day was, to which he replied "Tanks topped off" and walked out. That could mean but one thing - a deep penetration into Germany proper. We arose, washed ourselves in cold water, dressed and hurried to the hut in the hills. There we memorized the area, 10 miles in diameter surrounding the target, noting particularly road and stream junctions, overhead or underground bridges or railways, their location in respect to the target, prominent buildings, railroad Y's and sidings if any, extreme or noticeable bends in the river bank, groves of trees, and their shape, and many other small details that would enable us to find the target once we arrived in the immediate area of it. This is a very necessary procedure so that when we finally get there it will not be necessary to refer to any maps to determine where we are, for that we will know from our memory work which was done many hours before.

At 03:45 A.M. we returned to the Shack, awakened the pilot, Lt. Baker, and the Co-pilot, Lt. Chiles, and with them walked to the mess hall which was about one-half mile away. Breakfast as usual was very good and we ate heartily, knowing this would have to last until our return sometime late in the afternoon. During this time Lt. Baker and Lt. Chiles were busy quizzing us as to what the target for the day would be, and of course we refused to tell them anything except we had a full gas load with "tanks topped off." They could tell from this that in all probability it would be a deep penetration of Germany proper, for it was not customary to carry 'topped off tanks" unless going the extreme range of the bombers. However, at times we did do this to mislead ground crew members, as well as others who tried to outguess us as to where we might be going. In this business you can trust no one, except those actually involved, for the lives of many valuable men are at stake. It is indeed extremely dangerous to all concerned for it to become common knowledge where the target is, prior to actual arrival there. For the more who know it, the greater the chances that the Germans will find it out, and be waiting for us with all the fighters they have. This will not be very fortunate for the men who are to make the trip. As I think of it now I can't help thinking that someone talked that early morning, for we met a reception line such as had not been seen for months and would not be seen again until the close of the year, after the raids of the

11th and 18th. But enough of that for now and on with the story.

Upon completion of breakfast, which usually took 5 to 7 minutes, Lt. McGuinness and Sgt. Fischer, went to the Chapel where they received holy communion and we then made our way to the main briefing room where for the first time the remainder of the crew members would be enlightened as to what the target was, its location and actual take off time. At the door of the briefing room we were confronted with two rather sturdy looking M.P.'s, with a chart, and before being permitted to enter we had to give our crew number which was 13, the pilot's name and our names and respective positions on the crew. If all of this information corresponded with that on the M.P.'s list which had been issued him, entrance was permitted, otherwise it was forbidden. You could not attend a briefing, nor secure any data on a mission, unless you were making the trip yourself. Officers held their briefing in one building and the gunners held their briefing in another building, for different information is imparted to each group. Gunners were briefed on the type of enemy aircraft most likely to be encountered, the number they were apt to see, the various types of formation they would in all probability use in attacking, as well as the general area in which the planes would likely be found. The officers, myself included, were given this information, too. However, we did get much more, most of which is pertinent to specific duties on the ship and ours alone, and thus would prove relatively unimportant as well as confusing to the gunners. This included such data as assembly parts, flare colors for the day, control points and times, allied fighter support that could be expected, including type ships and number to be used, also the point and time they should be expected to join our bomber formation, weather data, exact route to be flown, distances and amount of time consumed, target arrival time, type of formation, our position in that formation, number of groups and wings participating in the raid, type of bomb carried, number and their weight, altitude to be flown on various legs, and numerous other things.

The main briefing consumed about a half hour, after which we were all dismissed to attend our special briefing session, the navigators, myself included, went to our room, to be issued maps, charts, logs and folders. Upon receipt of these the route was drawn in carefully to include all the logs. A straight course was never followed for this would necessitate flying over too many heavily fortified areas. By using the dog leg procedure most of them could be skirted, more often avoided entirely. I measured the length in miles of the various legs and figured the time that would be consumed covering them, taking into consideration the winds and temperatures most likely to be encountered at the altitude to be flown; next I was given the cities at which our fighter escort would intercept us, when they would leave us, etc. Of course, various points must be hit at definite times so often it was necessary to figure in reverse. This would enable me to tell the pilot what air speed he must fly to arrive right on time rather than too early or too late, either of which is not acceptable to the air corps. The time element is an all important factor and one that definitely can not be overlooked, for it is often the determining factor between a successful or an unsuccessful mission. So important, in fact, is this that all the crew members synchronize their watches to the second before leaving the briefing room. Seconds mean many miles, when traveling by air, as you will see later, so they can ill afford to be overlooked.

The bombardier, Lt. McGuinness, went to his special briefing room and worked some more on the target that had been selected. He also pondered over the secondary target, which would be bombed should some unforeseen difficulty prevent him from getting the primary one. It was not too often that this happened, but it did occur occasionally, and so he always found it wise to be prepared. I, as navigator too had prepared courses and distances to this secondary target, which I might be called upon to find in a minute's notice. Perhaps to you, my readers, this might sound like a menial task, but let me ask, "Do you think you could find a city you had

4

never seen before, into which there were no markers, and no radio to "home" in on?" If by chance you did find it, could you select the one building that was to receive your load of bombs, from all the rest that might be in the city? These cities ran all the way from a million to nine million in population. It is not easy and, of course, I wouldn't expect you to be able to do it, for you have not been given the training to do this specialized job, but even with the training it is not as easy as driving down the highway following the road signs.

The pilot, Lt. Baker, attended his briefing for a few last minute instructions regarding his position in the formation, and just what he was expected to do under various circumstances should they arise during the mission, as well as what responsibilities he was to assume.

The co-pilot, Lt. Chiles, had no further briefing, so checked on the "escape kits" for the entire crew and made his way out to the ship to see that it was in readiness for the proposed flight. He took special notice whether or not the gunners were getting their guns assembled and into position, which I might add was always very well taken care of by the gunners themselves, without any outside advice. They were vitally interested in their jobs and were even more interested in getting it done correctly for they knew full well that it would be they as well as the rest of the crew who would have to pay the penalty were it not correct. However, at times regardless of how well a job is done it is all to no avail, as we shall soon see. The gunners not only installed their own guns but also those for the bombardier and me. We were both still busy slaving over our maps, charts and targets for the day's mission and so had not arrived at the heartstand.

After working feverishly for twenty minutes, my map work had been completed, whereupon I packed everything into my brief case, and left the room. Entering the dressing room I again encountered Lt. Baker and Lt. McGuinness, who were in the process of dressing, and so I quickly followed suit, in order that we might all three be able to go out to the ship together. We all slipped on our heavy fur lined flying boots, stepped over to the parachute bin, and asked for our chutes, which we received immediately, and then left the building to make our way to the plane, via trucks that had been supplied by the squadron for that purpose. The plane was more than a mile from the briefing and dressing rooms, so it was nearly impossible to walk the distance, especially since we all had on our heavy clothing and our hands full.

In combat areas, it was always the policy to scatter the planes all over the field in heartstands, so as not to invite strafing by the enemy, which would be the case should they be lined up in neat rows along the runways. (We found that out the hard way on the disastrous attack at Pearl Harbor, and did not care to try it out again.)

After scrambling into the truck, with all our bulky equipment someone shouted, "Let her go," to which the driver immediately responded. He started the truck, turned on the lights and slowly moved down the still dark perimeter track, on either side of which could be seen the faint outlines of the high birds of destruction. Soon the pilots were calling out the numbers of the ships to which they had been assigned. "806" chirped Lt. Baker, as we made the first turn on the far corner of the field and in another few minutes the trucks pulled up to a heartstand and stopped. "Everyone off for 806," came a voice from the cab, so off we jumped, and on the driver sped to deliver the remaining men.

After placing our excess equipment in the ship, Lt. Baker carefully checked the ailerons, rudders, flaps, and landing gear, while the rest of us assembled and joshed one another about the day's work ahead, each trying to outdo the other describing how easy it was going to be. A great morale feature if nothing else.

In the meantime Sgt. Johannson and Sgt. Fischer began quizzing me as to the number of flak guns I expected at the target to which I hesitantly replied "700 or more," "far too many to be comfortable." This information I had secured at my briefing so it was not just a guess, but an actual computation of the number believed there, due to previous raids and area recognizance. This number of guns could quite successfully succeed in putting up a curtain so thick and black it would actually look like a severe thunder storm, but be many thousand times worse, for this cloud would be loaded with flying pieces of steel and shrapnel. This we must pass through once we arrived there. It was not a very pleasant thought to harbor, for go we must, so we just dropped the question right there.

Upon completion of the check Lt. Baker entered the ship through the escape hatch in the nose, crawled back to the bomb bay and surveyed the bomb load he was carrying. "Yep," there they were all right and beauties too, 500 lb'ers to be more exact. "They will surely make a dent when they fall," we heard him exclaim upon further examination. This remark, of course, brought to our minds an incident that had happened not so many days ago. It seems that we were supposed to bomb front line support at that, but due to the lack of those cherished explosives, we could not carry out our mission. This meant two things to us. First and most outstanding in our minds at the time was the poor fellows who were in the front lines eagerly awaiting our arrival so we might displace the heavy guns confronting them, thus permitting them to move forward without such a heavy toll in lives. Those boys died that day, for they were forced to do a job that we were expected to do, but could not, due to lack of bombs. Secondly, it created intense hatred in our hearts for those in the United States, the very people we were fighting for, who had fallen down on the job. They were engaged in a strike six months ago, when they should have been working, so now some of the finest men that America had ever produced, sons that mothers and fathers had devoted their lives to rear, were to lose their lives, because they could not get the proper support. The thought made us boiling mad, and I can still remember some of the statements that were made by various members of the crew: "What right does anyone have to deliberately cause the death of another person, unseen or otherwise, in the time of battle?" Some day, I trust those men who were responsible for these deaths, as well as the thousands and thousands of others who were sacrificed for similar reasons will be justly punished for their greed during an emergency. "No, I did not die, for I flew not, neither did my comrades on the base. We did not have the wherewithal to do the job, but we did think of the boys who would have to die as a result. They were our buddies, and we well knew just how it would feel to be in their places. The part that disturbed us more than any one other was that they probably breathed their last thinking that we, the air corps, had deserted them instead of those who had struck for "blood money" and preferred to be idle rather than help their country and fellow men in the midst of a dire emergency. What a disgrace, and what is even worse, what an unforgivable crime had been committed against the innocent boy who looked and prayed for help, but failed to receive it.

Chapter II
Take Off

"All aboard" came a voice from the cockpit window, so we broke up the discussion, jumped in, and all crawled to our respective positions, except Sgt. Gurman, the radio gunner, who brought each of us our interphone sets for the day's operation, after which he returned to his position. He also gave me my "flimsy." Take off time drew near and silent prayers were uttered by all of us while standing tense at our stations. The men gave a final check to their equipment, such as guns, oxygen supply, oxygen masks, interphone system, flak suit, parachute, electric heated suit, boots and helmet. Each officer in turn checked his special equipment using the prepared checklist, thus eliminating all chance of neglecting some important item, for once air-borne we must go on regardless of what might have been forgotten or misplaced, and this at times might prove very uncomfortable, or even disastrous for the entire crew, as the whole is no better than any one of its parts. I thoroughly checked my radio equipment, including the radio compass, the radar outfit, compass, altimeter, air speed indicator, temperature gauge, and a dozen and one other things, that always need the once over. Lt. McGuinness was busy checking his bomb sight, while over the interphone system I could hear the pilot calling off his list and the co-pilot, who was flicking switches to see if everything named by the pilot was in excellent condition, whereupon he slid back the cockpit window once more and called out "Clear One." He then proceeded to start the engine. The prop turned laboriously, jerkingly over, but soon the fuel ignited, and was spinning merrily. The ground crew man moved to the roar of engine No. II with his fire extinguisher and almost at the same moment Lt. Baker shouted, "Clear Two" and so another engine was set in motion. The same procedure was followed with engine No. III and No. IV and in another few minutes they were all humming merrily. He then started checking his "mags," oil pressure, gas supply and numerous other things that always need the final check, once the engines are running. By this time the entire field was humming with activity, for it was not only our ship that had started but fifty, sixty or even a hundred of the big birds, depending entirely upon the size of the raid that was to be carried out and the number of ships our group had been called upon to supply. The droning went to a higher pitch, hearts quickened even more, the plane lights were switched on, and they started creeping along the perimeter track over to their position on the runway. It was still dark as the sun had not yet pierced the eastern sky. The planes lined up on the end of the runway two abreast, one just a little behind the other so their wings might interlap. The pilots by this time had the engines revved up and were ready for the takeoff. There went the lead plane, 15 seconds elapsed – another made its way down the runway, and so it continued until all were airborne. You get no second chances in this game, you must be sure your ship is in condition before you get this far, for now there can be no holding up the procession or turning back.

It was our turn next, so Lt. Baker stepped on the brakes, pulled the throttles back, then released the brakes and we started down the runway. The airspeed indicator quivered-jumping back and forth—finally settling down to 100, gently easing forward and the tail rose from the ground, then 110...120...130...140...142...145. The pilot slowly eased the stick back, for we must become airborne. The end of the runway was right in front of us.

The ascent was gradual and very smooth, the touch of a skilled pilot. Airborne, we were climbing on the prescribed course at the briefed number of feet per minute, so there would be no chance of an accident while climbing to altitude. The fog was so thick that you could not see ten feet ahead. Flying weather such as we were experiencing that day, necessitated an instrument takeoff and ascent, and required really good pilots, with the know how plus lots of good judgement which comes only from conscientious training and hard work, many hours of practice, yes months and years of it previous to this time. A ship loaded with men, bombs and gasoline is nothing to experiment with but must be handled with care and caution, such as only an experienced pilot is capable of, and that kind of a pilot I am very happy to say we had, one of the finest that ever flew in the Eighth Air Force. I could never feel as much at ease, flying with any other.

In both the nose and the tail we had an "Aldus Lamp," flashing the group code signal. This rear one was operated by the tail gunner, Sgt. Fischer, and the one in the nose by Lt. McGuinness. The fog piercing light of the "Aldus Lamp" served as a warning to approaching aircraft, thus greatly reducing the hazard of a mid-air collision. We had been climbing for nearly thirty minutes on our triangular pattern when at last we broke through the fog, and so the signals were no longer needed, for now we could easily see the planes all lined up in their respective 15 second intervals, just as they had left the runway, more than a half hour before. A beautiful sight it was to behold, and to make it even more enchanting the sun was sending its first rays across the sky.

Upon reaching ten thousand feet the lead plane began making a big circle around the briefed "buncher" and while so doing shot his flares, indicating to the rest of us that he was now ready for us to assemble into our group formation positions. Lt. Baker promptly pulled up into high squadron lead by cutting across the circle and his wingmen soon followed suit. The formation was soon completed and we were on our way to make the first "time control point" good, which today was Landguard Point., a small jut of land just east of Ipswich, on the coast of England.

"Navigator to crew, Navigator to crew, if you will look below and a little to the right you will see Ipswich." "Our altitude is 11,000 feet and still climbing, temperature 7 degrees above zero."

At this point the pilot broke in "Pilot to crew, Pilot to crew, put on your oxygen masks, altitude 12,000 feet and going up." "Roger in the tail." "Roger in the waist." "Roger in the ball." "Roger in the Radio Room." "Engineer, Roger." "Roger in the nose," and so it went until all had reported in. By responding with the term "Roger," we assured Lt. Baker that we had heard his message and understood, and were doing as ordered, for to survive without oxygen from here on up would be an impossibility.

Landguard Point was just below us now, and we were right on time too, so everything had worked out to perfection. Taking up a heading of 87 degrees we turned out to the North Sea, and continued the climb phase, for we still were far below 26,000 feet. Shortly after heading over the North Sea, Lt. McGuinness punched his interphone mike button, and gave the crew instructions to test fire their guns, but to be careful not to hit any of the other ships in the formation while doing so. After handcharging the gun twice, the first round had made its way into the barrel, the safety switch was then flicked off, and worked the trigger. Fifteen rounds literally sailed through the gun before the finger could again be removed to stop it. The guns, were fifty caliber, fully automatic, and by simply pressing the trigger, and releasing it immediately, at least ten to fifteen rounds would pass through, so fast and smooth were their operation.

"Tail Gunner to Bombardier, Over."

Bombardier to tail gunner, "Go ahead."

Tail gunner to Bombardier, "Guns checked and found in order. Am connecting gun heater to prevent freezing."

Bombardier to tail gunner, "Roger, and out."

Soon all had called in and reported their guns in order, after which the interphone was again clear. We had been climbing all this time and had now reached 17,000 feet and were still going up at the rate of 300 feet per minute. Below us was nothing but the cold blue water of the North Sea, with an occasional harmless looking fishing schooner, while above was the clear blue sky with the sun shining brightly in the East. Another ten minutes and we were approaching the coast of Belgium, which was still in the hands of the Germans, and so could not be listed as friendly territory. Upon reaching 21,000 feet we found ourselves directly over the mouth of the Ghent River, from whence we made our way inland. Five thousand more feet and we would have reached our required altitude, and this was done in a matter of 17 minutes, after which Lt. Baker leveled off and retrimmed the ship, thus enabling him to maintain the 26,000 feet and fly along on a constant straight and level course.

"Bombardier to crew, Bombardier to crew, Oxygen."

"Okay in the tail," came the report from Sgt. Fischer.

"Okay in the waist," sounded off the waist gunner, Sgt. Rattin.

"Okay in the ball," reported the ball gunner, Sgt. Johannesen.

"Say, what the heck is the temperature; it's cold as _____ down here."

"Navigator to ball turret gunner, the temperature is 47° below zero."

"Freezing old top. Better turn up that thermostat on your electric suit if you are cold."

"Ball turret to navigator. Roger, and out old bean."

"Say, did you bring any cookies for me to eat when we get back to the North Sea?"

"Navigator to ball turret – Yes sir, Roy, one package, especially for you."

"Radio man Roger," shouted Sgt. Gurman, as though in a hurry.

"Engineer Roger," came the reply from Sgt. Damrel, the blonde curly haired Texan.

"Roger in the cockpit," chirped Lt. Baker as he went on checking his instruments.

As I was in the nose with the bombardier there was no need for me to send in a report for he could easily see that I was all right by simply turning around. Oxygen reports such as these are taken every ten or fifteen minutes, and if anyone neglects to answer he is immediately called again to see if he failed to hear the message, or what is the matter. If he does not respond on the second call a man is sent to his station, to ascertain just what the trouble might be. Either he has accidentally disconnected his interphone system, and not heard the call, or he has passed out from lack of oxygen, in which case he must have immediate first aid. The latter would not easily happen, but at rare intervals the connection on the oxygen mask pulls loose. If this should occur the man would die almost immediately, unless discovered. Before answering to the bombardier's call, all were always required to check their hose connection, and also the oxygen supply remaining, thus making certain that the former had not worked loose, and that the available supply of the latter had not run out.

Looking out of the window I could now see Brussels, Belgium and promptly notified the rest of the crew as to its whereabouts. It was easily distinguishable, for the sky was as clear as a newly washed window, giving unlimited visibility. Little did the crew know at that time that this was to be their last view of this great city. Little did we realize that we would never again see the English coast, the North Sea, the mouth of the Ghent, Brussels and all the other cities as they went by in machine gun order. We continued inland, and what before had been just a few harmless looking cumulus fair weather clouds, had now turned into a 50% coverage. However, it did not bother us too much for they were some 16,000 feet below. Occasionally they did succeed in blotting out the view of the landscape but only temporarily, for Lt. McGuinness was giving me pinpoint positions at the rate of one every five or ten minutes, thus indicating that he was finding his way through the coverage often enough to establish definite "air to ground" positions.

The gunners during all this time were busy scanning the skies for enemy aircraft, also watching the cities and rivers below us as we flew over them. When they saw a large city they did not recognize they would call me over the interphone, ask what it was, and I in turn would give them the information. By doing this they too helped in navigation, for the next time they saw this same city, they would call and tell me that it was either to the left or to the right, and I could then enter it on my log as a "pinpoint position." Besides this it kept them interested, and made their jobs educational, for they were learning place geography, and seeing first hand many of the cities that they had read about in their books while in school.

We headed southeast, and soon the Rhine River was below us and I wondered as we flew over it, just what the Germans were doing in the way of last minute defense preparations on the Siegfired to halt the onslaught of the huge allied war machine once it arrived. Could they stem the tide here, or would we pierce their defense like butter? However, I didn't wonder long for we had soon passed over it, and not too quickly either, for the place was bristling with anti-aircraft guns, and staying around any length of time might well nigh prove disastrous.

Section after section passed beneath us bringing new scenery and landscape, but still we kept going, on and on into what seemed infinity. Each second, each minute took us farther and farther away from home and allied hands, and deeper and deeper into Germany proper. It seemed there just was no end. Cologne had passed beneath us, as had the second target but for us there was no alternative, it must be the primary target if at all possible. If for some reason we could not get that, we would catch the secondary on the return trip.

Seconds passed into minutes, minutes into hours and still we continued on, east, southeast, east, forever onward into what now seemed eternity.

Would there be no end? It seemed not. To add to this discomfort were the elements, it was cold, bitterly cold, but there could be no turning back. We must go on—we dare not falter.

Two cities loomed up on the distant eastern horizon. Could one of them be it? No, it seemed hardly possible, for the target was still an hour away, which meant at least 180 miles more distance must be put between us and our allies. Not a happy thought, but it must be done.

Time for another regular ten minute entry into my log, so I proceeded to fill in the spaces. Time 11:45, wind direction 275 degrees, velocity 29 knots, position Leipzig to the right 21 miles Halle to the left, air speed 160 knots, ground speed 187 knots. Temperature 47 degrees, estimated time of arrival at target 12:35.

Here I was interrupted by the following interphone communication. "Engineer to crew, engineer to crew, I notice our fighter escort getting jittery, it appears they have spotted enemy aircraft in the vicinity, be on the alert."

Everyone now scanned the sky with renewed anxiety, and soon the report came in over the interphone.

"Tail gunner to crew, tail gunner to crew, I've spotted the enemy aircraft. They are between six and nine o'clock and coming in at us in wholesale lots." Enemy fighters are always called out by the time of the clock, figuring that 12 noon is the nose and that six o'clock is the tail of the ship. Then assuming that you are standing on the face of the clock you call them out by number, making it much easier to give a definite location, and also saves much valuable time. At the same time you also tell whether they are high or low, and they are located immediately by other members of the crew. We noticed our fighter escort jettison their auxiliary gas tanks and in a matter of minutes the battle was on in all its fury.

Chapter III
The Battle to Death

"Tail gunner to bombardier. They are coming in at us six abreast, and so fast I don't know which one to shoot at. There appears to be about a 15 second interval between fronts."

"Bombardier to tail gunner, Take it easy Fred, take it easy, just pick out one and concentrate on it until you get it preferably the center one."

"Bombardier to gunners, Train your guns on them and give those guys a case of lead poisoning they won't soon forget. Let's hit them with everything we got."

"Bombardier to radio man, Proceed to the waist and man your gun, it's now or never."

The bombardier was fire control officer, so had undisputed use of the interphone system, while under attack. He never waited for return answers, but just kept right on giving those orders he deemed necessary to good defensive gunnery.

By this time all eight guns that would point to the rear were firing relentlessly in that direction, while the four in the nose were shooting at the remaining planes as they skimmed beneath us. Few of them actually got to the nose but went streaking to the earth in a mass of flames as a result of "direct hits" by the gunners. The guns roared again, the ship trembled anew, and the battle increased in ferocity. "20 mm's," both shrapnel and incendiary were piercing our ship everywhere. How long could this go on? How much longer must we endure this strain? It seemed only our fighting spirit was holding us together now, and even that was rapidly ebbing away, for as I cast a glance at my ammunition box, I noticed the last 200 rounds were making their way into the chamber. Will they suffice? If not, what then?

At this point I decided it would be a very good idea to know my exact position just in case something drastic should happen for I had promised the crew I would give them this information should we ever be forced to bail. I picked up my navigation map of the area and was searching it intently when a 20 mm came through the nose and exploded right in the middle of it. Confetti was all that remained. I had a small bit in either hand but aside from that, NOTHING. The map had vanished into thin air and I had a deep shrapnel wound on the left hand. I looked out of the right window. One ship after the other was disintegrating in mid air, huge fortresses torn into pieces the size of silver dollars, and hurtling them earthward. What a few seconds before had been beautiful bombers with high-spirited crews, were now wrecks toppling to the earth.

Another roar, still another rumble, and the battle continued as chunks of metal flew in every direction. Our ship was dangerously crippled—20 mm's continued tearing through it from nose to tail. The bomb-bay area is burning profusely as a result of incendiaries fired into it. The tail has more holes than it had metal. Number three engine was gone. The waist was battered and ripped, the cockpit was in general disruption for the instruments have been shot out, and the nose took on the appearance of limburger cheese, with air pouring in from all directions.

It couldn't, it shouldn't, it mustn't go on I thought, but it did unrelentlessly. It seemed there was no end. All the surrounding bombers had gone down in flames and we were left to battle it out alone. How long could we last? Not long, but we went on fighting in spite of the odds. Did we give up? No, we did not! We had twelve 50's blazing with everything they had. We weren't cowards, we would fight it out to the finish and avenge our buddies' deaths, but in spite of our valiant efforts we soon lost the battle. Our ship made a sudden lunge to the right and up, as though going into a steep climb. I glanced out of the window, and noticed that our left wing had blown off just next to the engine. Now I became alarmed, so immediately removed my flak suit, and snapped on my parachute which was lying on the driftmeter just to my right. I had not been wearing it up to this time but felt the end had come and motioned to Lt. McGuinness to do the same, which he proceeded to do. It is virtually impossible to wear both the chest chute and the flak suit at the same time, so we must have a choice, and it is only natural that we chose the flak suit while under fire, for it would successfully deflect the larger portion of shells that hit that portion of the body which it covers, while the parachute would succeed in stopping nothing. Once I had the transfer made I tried to get to the escape hatch, but couldn't due to centrifugal force of the plane which was now out of control, so prayed for help as I knew this most assuredly was the finale. My entire life flashed before me in a matter of seconds, much like a runaway motion picture machine, and pointed out quite clearly all the compliments and favors I should have shown people for their kindness to me while still alive and able to do so, but now it was too late, for I had had my opportunity and failed. Death seemed a certainty, but I was now ready, for I had made peace with my God and so had no further qualms about it. The ship leveled off momentarily, gave another lunge and started into a dive. The right wing then blew off. This brought a last quick change in direction, heaved me headfirst into the "G-box" and knocked me out cold. I was to have destroyed the "G-box" with my foot, but by sheer accident I used my head instead. Seconds later the ship exploded tearing it to bits. The fire in the bomb bays had created such an intense heat that it succeeded in setting off the bombs, and so the coup de grace came to the last bomber of this 19 ship formation.

I remember the very instant of the explosion, for it seems that the concussion of the bombs going off gave me momentary consciousness, only to knock me out even colder. I distinctly recall a mass of flames, under terrific pressure hitting me in the face, no more. This then was the answer to my prayer. I had been released from the ship, totally unaware of it, along with the rest of the members and was falling to the earth 125 miles per hour – unconscious. How or where I blew out I do not know, nor for that matter do I have any idea just how my interphone and oxygen connections with the ship were severed for they were connected the last I remember. I fell more than 22,000 feet in this state, and upon coming to, noticed that I was somersaulting, at least assumed such as being the case, for one instant the earth was above and the next below, and I knew that was not normal. I immediately stiffened my body, taking it out of the limp form it had descended in and I found myself flat on my chest, descending in a horizontal position and this was most amazing for I thought surely it would be like diving from a board, either head first, or feet first, but such was not the case. I felt for my chute and found it still unopened on my chest, I would not dare open it while on my chest for if I did I would fall

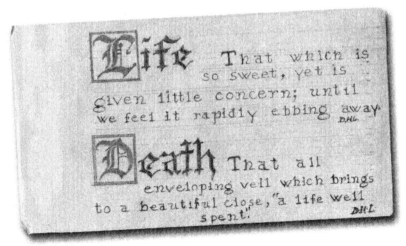

Prison camp diary entries created by the author as a POW, Barth, Germany.

Prison camp diary entries created
by the author as a POW, Barth, Germany.

right into it, and it would be of no value. I could see the tree boughs plainly by this time so gave my body a twist to the right and rolled over on my back. Then pulled the ripcord. I held on to the handle for a split second but realizing immediately that proof of jump here was silly, gave it a toss to the winds; I noticed three bodies lunge right on by me and fall into the forest, which I hit just 15 seconds later myself. Either they had not gained consciousness from the explosion, or had been killed in the battle that had ensued previous to it. I am certain that it was loss of consciousness with some of them for I positively know that not all received serious shrapnel wounds during the battle. As to the others, I can make no definite statement.

Fifty feet to the east, amidst the tall pine trees, lay the burning wreckage of a flying fortress. Several miles up and to the west I could see two chutes coming leisurely to the earth, but I had no time to concentrate on them for the present, rather must see to it that I missed the flaming fortress, into which the wind was sweeping me. Had it not been for the wind, it would have caused me little concern, but as it was I had to pull the shroud cords to my right and thus drift off in that direction, either that or fall into that flaming seething mass and go up in a pall of smoke. This I had no desire to do for my escape had been miraculous enough as it was. In another five seconds I was in the trees, and my worries were over. My chute had caught on the top of a tall dense pine, while I plunged on through the branches. I finally came to a halt about six inches from the ground. I immediately unsnapped my parachute harness and let myself down. Good old "Terra Firma" again after three miraculous escapes from death in the space of seconds. It seemed impossible, but had happened, God had been good to me.

Prison damp diary noting B-17 G tail number

Chapter IV
Attempted Escape

Immediate action at this time was a necessity, if I intended to escape and that I proposed to do if at all possible. It was very unlikely that anyone saw me parachute into the forest, for I had used the chute for such a few seconds, but there was an overwhelming possibility that they would send in a group of men to stamp out the conflagration that the blazing fortress had made, which was less than 30 feet from the spot where I was now standing. My parachute and harness were hopelessly entangled in the trees so I left them just where they were. I knew getting them down would consume more time than I could possibly afford at this moment, so I left them, hoping that the additional minutes gained would make a safe escape possible. I removed the first aid kit from the harness and shoved it into my pocket, then removed the "Mae West" (life preserver) that I was wearing, and threw it into the fire, at least destroying that much evidence. Next I removed my tie, for I was in need of a tourniquet for my injured left hand which was bleeding profusely from a shrapnel wound. There being nothing else that I wanted to get rid of this minute, I looked up to the sky, and offered a prayer of thanks. I then took a look at the sun and using it as a guide headed in a southwesterly direction toward Switzerland. After running for nearly a half-hour in the forest, I came to a paved road, which

I would have to cross to continue on my way. This I felt was extremely dangerous, for at most I could only be three miles from the scene of the accident. I had no doubt that the entire neighborhood was on the alert so I ran parallel to the road for a short distance, and finally found a tunnel. This I felt sure would solve the problem, so I bent down, crawled over to it, and passed under the road to the forest on the other side, where I again got up and started over hills and through the ditches. Thus I continued for the next hour and a half, stopping to walk only long enough to catch my breath, then running on. Soon I came to a very dense area, and as I was utterly exhausted, lay down to rest. After a few minutes had passed, I began to take a little closer look to see just what damage I had suffered as a result of the battle and found much to my amazement all portions of my face not covered during the explosion were burnt, eye lashes, and eye brows included. I then removed my leather helmet, which I was still wearing and found it full of blood. This set me to thinking, and plenty fast, for now I must decide whether to continue the escape plan, or give myself up and secure medical aid. I did not relish the idea of being captured for that meant imprisonment for the duration, and the more I thought of it the greater my dislike for it became. I patched myself up with the first aid kit as best I could and decided to let it go at that, at least until it got to the point where it was unbearable after which there would still be plenty of time to give myself up. I took off my flying boots, and hid them in the ground under a nearby stump, roots of which had rotted away. I also removed my navigator wings and buried them, for I had no intention of letting the Germans know what position I had on the ship, should they capture me, and that possibility did have to be considered, for I was just 60 some miles south of Berlin. I carefully concealed everything for I wished to leave no traces of the direction in which I was traveling. Next I removed my escape kit, that had been given to me by the co-pilot just prior to taking off, broke its seal, and took an inventory of the contents of the small packet. In it were maps of the area, and these I studied minutely, searching for my exact position. I also used them to compute the distance to Switzerland, and found it to be 270 miles at the place where I intended to cross the border. That shouldn't take me more than 19 days I said to myself. Why I'll be in Switzerland by my birthday! It was a pleasant thought. I further discovered that I was more than 350 miles from the nearest American lines and almost 600 miles from the nearest Russian lines. "Truly deep in the heart of Germany," with no visible means of defense, not even a knife. Upon completing the map work I began secreting the smaller articles in my clothing, eating several malt tablets during the process in an attempt to regain energy, for soon I was again to be on my way. A half-hour had elapsed, so I removed my heavy flying suit, wrapped it into a neat bundle, and again started out. I felt sure I could make better time carrying it for this would enable me to keep cool longer while running and then too I could have more freedom in movement. I was sorely tempted to bury it, however it was near the freezing point, and I knew that if I slept at all it would have to be outside, so kept it for my makeshift pajamas. It would also serve as a camouflage suit, for it blended in well with the green surroundings.

I traveled on through the forest perspiring profusely, and soon came upon a log cabin. I slowed down a bit and took a good look. It was apparently uninhabited, at least all outward appearances indicated such was the case, however, I couldn't be at all sure. Should I crawl through the clearing separating the cabin from me, and look into it further or should I go on? I decided to move on, for I noticed on closer observation that it had wires running to it, which undoubtedly were telephone wires, and if someone should happen to reside there they would most certainly discover me and notify the local authorities immediately. This I did not want to happen. After traveling several more miles I came upon a spring so I took out my small lister bag, filled it up, dropped in one of the purification tablets, and drank heartily, my first drink since early this morning and was it ever good! Wonderfully cool and refreshing!

This gave me added zest, but not for long, for as I came over the top of one of the wooded hills I ran upon a group of Germans, both men and women, working in the forest. I had seen them first so immediately threw myself down on the ground and cautiously crawled to the nearest thicket, which was a few hundred feet to my left. Here I had to stay until they left, for I was almost completely surrounded and back tracking would be virtually impossible. The chances of getting caught doing such a thing greatly outweighed those of remaining in the thicket, so I decided to "sweat" them out. In a half-hour or thereabouts the Germans left and the way was again clear for me to move onward.

The sun was setting in the west, but I continued on like a hunted deer, running a zigzag course and turning about periodically to see if I was being followed. Every crack of the trees startled me even more but I must continue on, weary though I was, for the more distance between me and that wreck before nightfall, the better my chances of escape. It was nearly dark now, so I began looking for a farm where I felt sure I could also find a hay stack or straw pile to sleep in without the occupant's knowledge. I came to the edge of the forest and there in the clearing, not a quarter of a mile away, was just what I had been seeking. "What a setup," I thought to myself, as I carefully sized up the situation.

Not a hundred feet away from the very spot where I was now lying was a potato patch. "Potatoes" I would have for dinner too, something that I had never planned on. Down by the barn, in a small lot were three milk cows. After dark, fresh milk! I would milk into my lister bag, drink it, and then fill it up again. This got better by the minute, and the longer I waited for total darkness the harder it became to lie still. I heard voices in the distance. They drew nearer. Now I could hear them wailing "NO! NO!" I said, "Please God, don't let them discover me now," but all to no avail. They continued on, and were bound to step right on me unless they changed their direction. I could see the dim outline of a six year old boy and eight year old girl coming toward me, but there was no stopping them. The only thing I could do was lie perfectly still, and hope they didn't stumble over me, for to move now, would mean sure discovery. I lay there, my heart began to pound – louder and louder it grew – 'til it sounded like a truck. In a few seconds I would know the answer. They stepped right on me, screamed to the top of their childlike voices, went running down the incline to their home which was in the village below, still yelling for all they were worth. I could easily have grabbed the children and strangled them, but this was against my principles. I got up, ran uphill into the forest, and had not been in it a minute, when the church bells and the sirens in the village blew. This signal indicated that enemy airmen were in the immediate district, and everyone should set out in search of them. I am not so sure about the "men" but I do know there was a "man" present, and that man lost no time in throwing his plans overboard and getting deeper and deeper into the forest. I had run for nearly an hour when I came upon a tank, in a small cleared area, I took off my helmet, stuck my face in it, and drank. After filling up, I plunged my entire head in to cool off, and then started out anew. The Germans were combing the forest area below me and that meant I must get out. It was now or never! I looked up to the sky took a look at the stars and singled out Polaris. Then I went on down the handle of the Big Dipper until I came to "Spica." This was to be my guide, for I could see it through the top of the trees, and by following it I would be going south and west and so would at least get closer to my goal. Furthermore it eliminated the necessity of getting out my small compass, which would take time, and I had none of that to spare at this moment.

I continued my travels during the greater part of the night stopping occasionally to get a drink from the springs as I ran across them. Five hours had elapsed since my last rest, and I just could go on no longer. My legs were weak, and my feet felt like lead. I could not hold out no matter what happened. If they caught me, let them. I just could not go any longer in my present tired condition. I forged ahead to a very dense area, got down on my hands and knees, and crawled into it. Here I lay down, and tried to sleep, but try as I may I could not.

I could hear twigs crackling, indicating the hunt was still going on, then I smelt smoke, which I imagined came from a cigarette. Was it another American who had gotten away? Or was it the Germans still searching? I never succeeded in finding out, for after lying there for a half hour, twisting and turning I could stand the uncertainty no longer, so again started on the move. Tired as I was I managed to struggle along, but at a considerably slower pace than heretofore. Occasionally I would take malt tablets from my escape kit, to supply me with quick energy, but I was doing my level best to conserve them, for I knew that this was just the beginning of a rather extensive journey.

Morning found me still plodding away over the now mountainous timber area. Some of the timbers had had the underbrush trimmed out, while other areas were so dense it was necessary to put my arms in front of me while walking to protect my burnt face. My scalp wound had clotted over, and so no longer gave me any alarm, but the left hand still was in rather bad condition. It did not appear to be getting any worse, so I decided to continue on.

I had gone about two hours when I came upon a red raspberry patch on the sidehill of an apparently uninhabited bluff. "Breakfast" I thought, "if only I am not disturbed." I commenced picking them, first one at a time, but soon by the handful, for I was extremely hungry. I ate about two quarts of them, while crawling through the patch on my stomach, and proceeded onward. Now at least my stomach walls were not rubbing together for lack of food.

Up one peak and down the other I went, for I didn't dare follow the road in the valley below. I could see the Germans working in their fields and small shops, but nearly always stayed far enough in the woodland so I would not be discovered. I was gaining more confidence, and getting a bit bolder, for things had gone well for some time now, and just as I was about to walk over the top of a peak what should I see but a dozen Germans. What they were doing, I do not know, I only knew that I threw myself to the ground and started crawling down the same side I had just spent an hour coming up. Then I circumnavigated them by taking a northern route. This was definitely against my principles, for I wanted to either go south or west all the time, but to do it now, was an impossibility for it necessitated crossing a well traveled paved road, and to do that in broad daylight, was taking too much of a chance. I succeeded in getting around them, and had no more than done so, when I ran into a potato patch. This time I meant to get some. I crawled over the grass in my flying suit and soon arrived at my destination. I dug down beside the plants and helped myself for they were free for the taking. I took about eight and again crawled back to the timber, where I cleaned them up. I ate them raw, for I knew they contained starch, and as I remembered, starch would turn to sugar, and sugar would supply me with energy. So I was happy again and partially filled too. I had not forgotten my recent escape though, and so proceeded more cautiously. On and on I went, through one forest after the other, down paths and over hills. The sun had passed its zenith, and was again making its way to the west. I came in sight of some more Germans, and in order to circumnavigate them it was necessary for me to again crawl through a potato patch. I proceeded to do so and had gotten half way through when a dog, either saw me moving in my green suit which matched almost perfectly with the potatoes or smelled me and began to bark! First his master paid him no heed. The dog drew closer and grew more persistent by the minute. Again his master called him but the dog refused to budge. He finally came up the ledge and took a look himself. He searched carefully, but failed to see me, and so returned to his gardening, taking the dog with him. What a relief. Again I had been spared, but how much longer could this go on? Had it not been for the near perfect blending with my surroundings I most assuredly would have been discovered. I vied with the ground to see if I couldn't displace it, so close was I hugging it for dear life. I waited another fifteen minutes until things quieted down a bit and feeling sure the dog had forgotten me, started crawling to the other end, into the forest. What an escape that was, and in broad daylight too! I didn't care for many more of those, for they were rather hard on my already shaky nerves.

Several hours later I came upon a grain field. The sheaves of grain had been hauled to one corner and shocked in neat rows. One shock was right beside the other. This I reasoned would make an ideal spot to hide out, for to find me at all they would have to stumble almost on top of me. This seemed highly unlikely for there was no one around the area. then too the straw would make a warm mattress on which to lie in the sun. So I fashioned myself a mattress and lay down between the rows in the nice warm sun and promptly fell into a deep sleep. Complete exhaustion had hit me and I could no longer resist.

Chapter V
Capture

About an hour later I was rudely awakened by three Gestapo agents with machine pistols in their hands. "The jig was up." I had had my fling at escape and failed. How they happened to discover me I'll never know, but it is my belief that some farmer accidentally walked by and saw me sleeping. Knowing he couldn't take me alone, he went for aid. He couldn't have selected a tougher outfit, the most murderous gang in all of Germany. My fate was sealed.

"Hands up," they said in German. I stirred not a muscle, for I acted as though I did not understand their language. They reiterated their command. I still didn't move. They raised their guns, and my hands moved slowly upward, but they soon made up my mind for me. One of them stepped forward with his machine pistol, and as I stared down the business end of that gun hesitancy grew into haste. Two slugs out of that and I would be out forever, and it wasn't just the one before me that set me to thinking, but the two backing him up – with the same type guns. He frisked me and we marched off.

All the way to the city, which lay between two fairly good sized mountains, they kept questioning me as to what happened to my comrades, but I remained mute, for I decided I would not be an information bureau.

Right down main street we went, one beside me, and two behind, to make sure I stayed in line. The villagers all came from their homes and shops to witness the spectacle. Some jeered, others shook their fists, some laughed in mockery, while still others stood quietly by completely motionless. Mixed emotions, if I had ever seen them. The children followed on down the street behind me, as though I were the Pied Piper of Hamlin. What a sensation I was creating in this city. Upon arrival at headquarters I was whisked inside and the crowd soon dispersed.

"Take off your clothes" said the chief in German. I didn't budge! I was determined not to let them know I understood German, but it seemed I had better dispense with that idea, and center more attention on my life, which by this time was hanging on a shoestring. They were becoming violently angry, this I knew, for they were flushed in the face. I further knew that if I refused to carry out their orders they could shoot me and be perfectly within their rights, for the Geneva Convention regulations specifically state that you must carry out all orders given to you by your captors. I did not remember for sure whether they were supposed to be given in a language you understood or not, but rather than quibble over the point and lose my life, which I valued quite highly, I conceded and did as he commanded. I knew I could not shorten it at any rate, for these men definitely understood no English, nor did they speak it, and if I had any idea of getting out of this place alive it was either to act or to be a dead pigeon. I chose to act, without further hesitation.

I removed my clothes, every stitch of them, I then stood over in the corner under guard of the chief's companions, while he carefully searched them. My, what he didn't find! It's amazing! Hack saw, compasses, maps, French Francs, potatoes, small razor, sewing kit, first aid kit, malt tablets, etc. I was well aware that I had all these things, for they were the very articles I had secreted in my clothes while resting in the forest. He really did a very thorough job, and got everything with the exception of one compass. They even searched between my toes, my mouth, ears, hair and nose. "Never missed a lick."

Now the trouble began. I did not mind them confiscating those articles that I knew in my own mind I was not to have on my person, but when they started taking my rank, collar insignia, dog tags, fountain pen and pencil set, religious medal as well as crash bracelet, that was too much. I wouldn't have it, so walked up to the desk, picked the articles up and put them in my pockets. They promptly removed them again. I told the chief in the best German I could muster for the occasion and the strongest too "according to the Geneva Convention regulations, you are not permitted to take these things from me, and I wish to keep them." I picked them up again and was about to put them in my pocket, when the chief drew his gun. I labored under the assumption that he meant business. "We intend to keep those articles whether you like it or not" he said in German. "They shall be prizes of war." That settled it. He kept the religious medal and all. I had been to the cleaners, and come out second best. At this point he began his interrogation.

"What is your name?"

"Donald H. Lienemann, Sir."

"What is your serial number?"

"0-717607, Sir."

"When were you born?"

"Sir, I refuse to answer that question."

"What do you mean you refuse to answer?"

"Sir, I am required by the Geneva Convention to give you only my name, rank and serial number. That I have done, and that is all you will get."

"What group do you belong to?"

No answer.

"Were you based in France?"

Having found nothing but French money on my person during the search must have prompted this question, but I gave him no satisfaction. I left him to draw his own conclusions, saying nothing.

"Still no answer." "Where are your comrades?"

Yes, a very good question, and I should like to know the answer to that myself, but still I said nothing.

"Either you answer those questions or into jail you go, and you'll stay there until you decide to talk."

No answer, so he threw me bodily into the nearest cell.

Now, I was in jail for the first time in my life. "Homey?" I am afraid not. What a filthy hole. It looked as though it had not been cleaned for years, and probably had not either. I had as my companions, bugs of every size, shape and description, plenty of dirt and a wooden bench. It looked and smelled like a dungeon, but I did not bother with that for the present, rather concentrated on getting out. I checked the bars on the outside window, which I found to be 1 inch solid steel. I tried them, they refused to budge. Pretty substantial. Then I checked the masonry, now there was an angle, if I were in here for the night – say – well I might be able to work out something. Already it was growing dark, but not dark enough for that. If I should succeed in getting out, what would I do for shoes? These they had kept outside my door. I might steal a pair, but first I must get out. I sat down on the bench and reflected on all that had happened during the past two days. It seemed a lifetime had come and gone those forty eight hours, but such could not be and I knew it only too well. I thought too of how clean the forest had been through which had passed, not a twig or dead stick was to be found anywhere, unless it was one that had just recently fallen down, and even those were rarities. It was nothing short of amazing how meticulously clean they kept them and it seemed unbelievable, but such had been the case. After an hour of such meditation the guard came to the door and took me out, so that stopped my trend of thought and solved my escape problem right there and without further ado I was being moved. I put on my shoes, and was led to the street. Here I was confronted with another American who had been shot in the foot. He was very friendly, but I refused to talk to him, for I had no way of knowing who he was, or for that matter whether he actually was an American or not. He might be a German dressed in American clothes. How was I to know? I knew they had our uniforms, for they had kept both my flying suit and jacket. What more proof did I need than that? If he did prove to be an American I would find it out soon enough. The Germans were very shrewd, and pulled all kinds of stunts to get information and not wishing to be taken in by them, or one of their tricks, I kept my mouth shut. They had secured no information and were to get none if I could help it. They gave me orders to help the injured man down the street, to the depot, and this I did, semi-carrying him on my back. He weighed more than I did and proved to be quite a load, but with a gun prodding me along I made the grade, only to arrive at the station completely exhausted. I sat down on the appointed bench and waited for the train. It came and backed in, from the southeast. Strange way to get a train into town, but when the tracks do not run through it how else can it be done?

"Hurry up," shouted the trainman, as though in haste, so we clambered on. The train gave a jerk, and we were under way. Where to was anybody's guess. Where I had been was even unknown to me at this time, but I had taken enough mental notes to be sure I could find it once I got a good map. I noticed as we left the city the train came in on a "Y" and headed west, southwest. This I could tell by looking at the stars, for I was sitting next to the window and watched them closely as we moved along. We came by a city that had been bombed during the afternoon, and I attempted to take a look out of the window and see what destruction had been done, but I was promptly slapped in the face by the Gestapo agent sitting right across from me. Had he known I was watching the stars between the cities, thus determining direction, he would in all probability have stopped that too. He apparently was so sure I could see nothing of any value that he didn't bother to stop me. For that much I was indeed thankful, for sooner or later I would find out where I had been captured.

The ride took about three hours and was uneventful, other than the slapping or two that I received, which was not too bad considering what might have happened instead. I almost froze, due to the lack of my jacket, which the Gestapo had confiscated. But I assume a few goose pimples are unimportant and not too damaging. We deboarded and made our way along the station platform to the local police headquarters. While walking along we encountered several old German women carrying huge sacks on their backs containing what looked like potatoes or apples. Several of them got in our way, and the Gestapo agent, rather than walk around them just shoved them aside. They fell in a heap on the brick pavement with their loaded pack. It seemed a shame, even to me, that these people should be treated in such an ill manner by one of their own, but apparently the Gestapo had little respect for anyone, except themselves. They were killers and there were no two ways about it. I thought I will be only too happy to get out of their hands into those of a more respectable branch, and I hope it happens soon, for it is doubtful if they will fool around with me much longer.

Upon arrival at the station the agent turned me, and the other wounded man, both over to the Luftwaffe authorities, and left. I can not remember the time I've been so glad to get rid of a man in my life. I only hoped he'd break his neck before he got back to wherever he might be going.

I asked for first aid to my injured hand. I thought perhaps these men might have a heart, but no help was forthcoming. The wounded gunner asked for the same for his foot, and got the same reply. It seemed they did not much care whether we got help or not. They loaded us in a truck and drove us off to an airfield under the able guard of two trusty men with submachine guns. Upon arrival we were ushered upstairs and interrogation number two began. They started in on the enlisted man and every time he was about to answer some question he shouldn't I stopped him, telling him that the convention regulations did not require that. This became very annoying to the interrogator so he had me removed from the office, but not before I gave the man direct orders not to give any information except his name, rank and serial number. The interrogator gave me a sharp tongue, a nasty look, and into the next room I went. I was nearly shot over the deal, but felt it my duty as an officer to stop him even at the cost of my life. Here I sat for an hour and a half still under the guard of those two huskies with submachine guns. Where I had acquired such a bad reputation I don't know, but they had no intention of letting me get away, I could see that. Perhaps the lack of information disturbed them but whatever it was, this was helping matters none, for now I was more convinced than ever that they would get no information from me. Whether they secured any information from him, I do not know for I was unable to hear. I know he could tell them nothing about me, for he didn't know me, and I had told him nothing, not even when or where I was shot down, and didn't intend to. They finally rapped on the door, called me back in and commenced the interrogation. We started out asking the routine questions, and of course I answered the first three, name, rank and serial number. Then I stopped.

"What is the matter, don't you want to leave here," he inquired?

"Sir, I'll rot here before I give you any more information."

That was a good question wasn't it? But it could only be answered one way. The truth, either they believed it or they didn't.

"Sir, I have no proof. The Gestapo took my identification bracelet, and dog tags, both—you will have to take my word for it."

"We don't take anybody's word for anything," he retorted. "But if you tell us to what group and squadron you belonged, and from what base you flew, then we can determine who you are."

"Sir, I refuse to divulge that information, for according to the Geneva Convention regulations I am not required to give you anything but name, rank and serial number. Those you have and that is all you get."

"The Gestapo took my dog tags over the point of a machine pistol, you can blame them for that."

"Do you need first aid?"

He could see that I did, that is precisely why he asked so, I answered "yes."

"If you will tell me what I want to know I will see to it that you get the required medical attention, otherwise you will do without."

"Huh, I thought, so they bribe you too, do they?" They will stoop to most anything. Well, I've gotten along this far without help, and would rather die than take advantage of this "blood gesture," I remained mute.

"Where were you captured?"

"I don't know, sir, they did not tell me the name of the city." I didn't either, so really had told them the truth, for it was not until I got back to England, after release from prison camp that I actually found out.

"Why didn't you look for signs?"

Actually all the signs had been removed, and they knew that too. It was a catch question, so I said nothing, for I saw this was getting me nowhere fast. I continued this "mum" attitude and finally it annoyed him to the point of utter disgust.

"You see this blank," he said holding it up for my inspection. "You must give me enough information to fill it out completely or stay right here and not ship out with your comrade."

Now, wasn't that some alternative to give me? After all what difference did it make whether I was held here or somewhere else? I would be a prisoner of the Germans in either case. Secondly, I didn't know the other man, so what! "Sir," I replied after due deliberation, "you are going to have a long time boarder, if I have to give you that information." That settled that, for I was taken to the basement and put into solitary confinement, pronto. Later they gave me half a bowl of soup and three cooked potatoes.

This food was very welcome indeed, for I had not eaten for nearly twelve hours. Nor had I had anything to drink. I ate heartily, as long as it lasted, then fluffed up my straw mattress and lay down on the wooden bench. My back was frightfully stiff, and it nearly killed me to bend it, but bend it I must if I intended to lie down. The cellblock was everything but comfortable, for all it had was a wooden stool, plus the wooden bench I was lying on. Exceedingly empty, but I was thankful even for that, for I was indeed lucky to be alive, which was a lot better than most of my crewmates had fared. I still had life, health, and had lost none of my appendages, even though one was seriously injured, so had few complaints to offer. I offered a prayer of thanks to God that I had been spared and delivered this far safely and asked for His continued guidance in the days to come after which I rolled over and went to sleep. I was dead tired, I hardly noticed the hard bench, but slept undisturbed until morning, only to wake up with an even stiffer back. I arose, moved the wooden stool over to the small window on the outside wall, clambered up and took a look. There was very little to see but at least I could get a view of the general surroundings. I noticed they had a two-foot thick barrier of crushed rock up along the side of the building, held in place by a network of vertical poles. Either the outside walls of this place were none too substantial and this had been put here to prevent a mass outbreak, or it was a safeguard to prevent bomb damage, should one drop close by, and that was entirely possible, for the airfield was just one-half mile down the road. I would hear the fighters warming up during various hours of the day, especially right after an air raid alert had been sounded. It must be breakfast time, I thought to myself, for it has been light for several hours already. But no, I was mistaken – not in the time of the day, but the service. There would be no food, no water, no nothing. Apparently they were going to carry out their threat, and see if I would give in, at least they had made a good start. About ten o'clock a guard came to my door, after considerable key dangling, opened it. He pretended that he could speak very little English, and in broken tone would keep repeating "Chiles," "Chiles," "Chiles." I recognized what he was saying all right, and wondered what was up, but acted dumb. I didn't care to give him any indication that I knew such a person. You will remember he was the co-pilot, and was mentioned earlier in the story. Finally he turned around and locked the door, all the time muttering to himself, something to the effect that I must not have recognized the name, for I gave him no indication. It made me happy to think that they had not succeeded in tricking me, but at the same time I became a little disturbed. Had they captured Chiles? If so, where was he?" Could it by any chance be that he was in the same building? If so, had he talked, or had he too refused to give any information regarding himself, and the crew? The more I thought about it the more disturbed I became. Maybe they did know more about me than I thought, but were just kidding me along. I rather doubted that though, for had it been the case they most assuredly would have told me during the interrogation, just to get my instant reaction. They would not trick me up now though, for I would prepare myself, and act perfectly nonchalant. Further worry over it would do no good at this time so after figuring out an angle of self-protection, I lay back on the tow sack filled with straw, and rested my lame back.

Noon, and again the tinkle of keys could be heard down the hall. I went to the door and peered out of the small one-inch hole that had been drilled into for a peephole. The guard was coming down the hall opening each of the cells as he came. I wondered what was up, and found it to be lunchtime. One-half bowl of barley soup and a slice of bread were the rations, and they were most welcome, for I was nearly famished. Upon completion of the snack, I stepped out into the hall and there to my amazement stood Lt. Chiles just four cells down. I said nothing, much as I wanted to, didn't even give him a second glance. To do so would serve only to give him a second glance. To do so would serve only to give us both away. I must wait until some time later when it wouldn't be quite so obvious, sometime when we were herded into a group, and it would only be natural that we talked, whether we knew the person or not. My anxiety nearly got the best of me, but in spite of how bad I wanted to know, I did an about face and walked back into the cell. There was another thing in that hallway though that did particularly intrigue me. It was a small fellow about 15 years old, dressed in Russian uniform. He spoke fluent Russian, German and English, and did his best to talk to everyone of us during the period our cells were open. His prime interest seemed to be what had happened, where, and who our crew members were. He said that he had been here 18 months, which sounded very fishy indeed, for usually no one stayed over one or two days at the most. He was general "flunky" and washed the bowls and spoons after we had finished with them thus furnishing him the excuse to enter the cell. Although I have no definite proof, I would say he was a stool pigeon, placed here by the Germans to secure whatever information he could, regarding any of us. I felt this from the very beginning, and so said nothing to him, I had made a firm resolve not to tell anything to anyone when captured, and meant to keep it to the letter. That I was sure would be the best way to prevent being tricked, or caught in one of their very cleverly laid plots. They find it very difficult to catch you off guard if you don't say anything at all, so "mum" was my password, and would be until I got back home where I knew I could trust those to whom I talked. It was not even safe to talk to yourself in the cell or anywhere for that matter, for microphones were secreted all over the place. The only safe thing to do was to think to yourself, for it was doubtful if they had mental telepathy down to a science.

During the afternoon the German Major paid me a visit asking me if I had changed my mind and was now ready to talk, to which I answered a polite "No sir."

"In that case you leave me no alternative, you will stay here and live on bread and water. Your comrades will be shipped on to better quarters."

This was something to think about, not the quarters, but the fact that Lt. Chiles might leave without my ever getting to see him again. Nope, I wouldn't weaken now, I'd take that chance. Things always happen for the best.

"Yes Sir," I answered, and he departed hastily as he came. Disgruntled, no doubt for he failed again.

For dinner we had two slabs of sour black bread after which the lights were turned out, so I retired for the second night only to be awakened at midnight by the tinkle of keys, and lights. Now what was up? They were moving some of the men out as they had promised they world. This was the crisis, either I would or I wouldn't. There could be no half-way mark here. He kept working his way down the hall and was soon unlocking the door just across the hall. Would he turn around and unlock mine? That was the "64 dollar question!" He turned slowly around, hesitated, then looked at the list he had in his hand, and came to my door. Now I could breathe easier, for in a matter of seconds he had it opened, and told me to get out. I was moving.

What a relief and what a bunch of liars they turned out to be. However, I was very glad it turned out that way, for this might give me the chance I had been waiting for – to talk to Lt. Chiles. We were marched out and loaded into a truck, and hauled to the railroad station. The train was late, so they told us to go ahead and sit down, which we all did right in the middle of the station. They surrounded us with guards, but at least we were free to talk, and as luck would have it I found myself right next to Lt. Chiles. Did I dare risk talking to him" Or should I wait" I wondered, I hesitated. Evidently he was doing the same thing for he didn't say a word. Neither of us had made any special moves to get in these positions, it just happened, so in that respect it ought to be safe. But then, there was the thought they would notice we were quite chummy, once we began our chat, and draw unwarranted conclusions. This would definitely be bad, for as yet we had not been to the main interrogation center we had heard so much about while still free men, Stalag Luft I, located at Frankfurt. Should I risk it" No, it seemed hardly worthwhile, so I postponed it again. How much longer I could satisfy my curiosity by good logical reasoning was questionable, but at least I had won this time. Let the next time take care of itself whenever it arose. For five hours we sat there, looked at each other in wondering glances, and said nothing. Truly a trying experience. After which the train made its way into the station, and we were again under way. Where to, or how long the trip would take, no one knew. I did know that we were headed west, other than that my mind was a total blank as to location. This time there wasn't even a good way to take mental notes on where I had been for there wasn't a thing unusual about the place. To this day I am without the answer to that problem. All day we traveled by train with no opportunities to visit, and still less to eat. But by this time it was becoming commonplace to go on a thin diet, so I thought little about the situation. We did manage to get a drink of water in one of the stations while changing trains, so didn't suffer in that respect. Several times the guards tried getting coffee for us from the German Red Cross Canteens, which were operating in the stations, but were unsuccessful in all but one attempt. In that one single instance we received one cup per individual, for which we thanked them from the bottom of our hearts in German. All the boys had learned to say "Thank you" in German by this time, and it pleased the ladies very much, for they left with smiles on their faces. While passing through the stations we could not help noticing the Russian women slave laborers they were using to clean up their litter. They were stooping over picking up the filth and sticks from between the crushed rock road bed. Few if any were under fifty, and it was an appalling situation, but such were the ways of the victor. The Nazi, SS and Gestapo heels had born fruit!

We reached our destination by nightfall and after being taken from the train we were marched a half mile to the street railway system. The trolley pulled up, but was so crowded that the guards decided it best to wait for the next one. They didn't care to mix us with the civilians, for they knew fights would result, and as both of them were fairly jammed, told the conductor to go on.

This then was the moment for which I had been waiting. Out in the wide open spaces, no microphones around, no interference from anyone. It was dark, so for them to detect who I was talking to would indeed be difficult if not impossible. What a chance to talk to Lt. Chiles. The guards stood at least forty to fifty feet away, and had us surrounded, so escape was out of the question. I walked up to Lt. Chiles, and told him how glad I was to see him, he in turn did the same. Immediately thereafter we delved into the fate of our still missing crew members, which were seven in number. During the course of the conversation he related to me what he knew had happened in the ship prior to his leaving it, and in order to clarify the story I shall now relate it to you.

Both Lt. Chiles and Sgt. Damrel noticed the fire in the bomb bays during the pitched battle that was taking place in the air. Sgt. Damrel, the engineer, stood right in front of the area and was being burned around the legs. He left his guns and grabbed the fire extinguisher, in an attempt to extinguish the blaze, but all to no avail, for it was burning so intensely that it only seemed to fume up in greater anger. However, in spite of this he continued with all the courage he could muster. Lt. Chiles, upon noticing the fire, took the interphone and tried to call the crew, telling them the ship was in a dangerous state, and would have to be abandoned. He explained to me that he tried every position on the switch, but none of them worked. The interphone had been completely shot out, as had the instrument panel and "C I" (automatic pilot). He next tried the alarm bell, which is the automatic signal to bail. It too failed to ring. He then nudged the pilot, Lt. Baker, and told him about the situation. Lt. Baker took one look around, and gave both Lt. Chiles and Sgt. Damrel verbal orders to bail out, which they proceeded to do without further questions. By this time the extinguisher was empty and the fire was burning with even greater intensity. Lt. Baker apparently then made a momentous decision. Rather than bail out and save his own life, he decided he would stay with the ship, in the hope that the rest of his crew members would find out about the fire and bail out on their own initiative, without first waiting for his instructions to do so. He stayed – knowing full well that in a matter of seconds he was going to give everything he had, even life itself, for his crew members whom he loved so dearly. He must have felt that those few extra seconds, he was now so unselfishly giving might help another to get out safely, and survive the fatal blow that was sure to come. More unstintingly, I dare say, no man has ever given for his country, or fellow men. For this he was to receive no medal, no glory, but only certain sure death. It didn't seem fair! But so attached to his crew had he become that he would not do otherwise. He went to his death, a truly great man. Greater devotion had no man for his crew, and a better pilot is yet to be born.

Those two chutes then, that I saw must have been Sgt. Damrel and Lt. Chiles. But what had happened to Damrel? Neither of us knew for he had not been seen since. He left the plane, that was certain. After that, well only time would supply the answer.

That left five men still unaccounted for, but the story is not yet finished. He further related to me that he had been shown the dog tags of Sgt. Johannesen, which were all bent up and bathed in blood. This during his first interrogation by the Germans. These, they related to him came from a man who had plummeted to earth in a metal ball. It is highly likely that such was the case for when the ship blew up, it in all probability freed the ball turret, and in it Sgt. Johannesen went to his death, for from it there was no means of escape. This was indeed a shame for he was a grand fellow – the favorite of the crew – a better gunner, or more sincere man I've never known.

Besides this, he had been shown Sgt. Gurman's dog tags, and they were in the same general condition. These, they related had been taken from a gunner they found lying dead in the woods. This too was entirely possible, and undoubtedly true, for I had seen three men fall into the trees without opening their chutes. He most assuredly was one, and was released from the plane at the same time I was, however, he never regained consciousness to open that life saving chute. The finest radio man in the business too had gone the way of all life.

The manner in which the score was adding up was definitely not very pleasant, and now I commenced to wonder why I was so anxious to talk to Lt. Chiles at all. But sooner or later the truth would have to come, so just as well now as in the indefinite future.

At this point our little session was broken up by the guards, for they thought we were plotting some scheme to escape them in the darkness. At least I had partially satisfied my curiosity, and the rest would have to wait, until another opportunity presented itself. I had about all I could stand for the present anyway.

They watched us very closely so that we did not mingle with the civilian population, nor they with us. It seemed that the civilians of this area had a particularly intense hatred for "Airmen." To me, this was rather hard to understand, for hadn't their pilots been guilty of doing the same things we had just completed? Didn't they start all this aerial warfare on completely defenseless nations? Were they not responsible for the mass murders of innocent civilians in occupied countries? Or were they so blinded by Nazi propaganda, they didn't know? Surely they must be fully aware that many of their boys fly away each day never to return. Didn't they know that they fell into Allied hands, just as we fell into German hands? Weren't they just as guilty of murder as they accused us of being? If so, they certainly could not see it. They would step up to us as near as they dared, for the guards made them keep a reasonable distance away, shouting, "Murderers" "Baby killers," "Gangsters" in plain English. This was most amazing and I couldn't for the life of me figure out where they had learned such words, but on quizzing the guards later, I found the answer. German propaganda, newspapers to them had told them that the entire air force of the United States is composed of released Chicago gangsters, who had been instructed to rain death and destruction on the German people, especially the civilians. If a thorough enough job were done their past records would be wiped out, and they could start anew. What vicious lies, but it had the desired effect, even though we all knew it was a far cry from the truth. Every day the radio would blare out that more gangsters were on the way, and that they should take the proper precautions. As they were not permitted to listen to any other stations than those in Germany, their minds soon became warped. Some of them would risk listening anyway, but once they were caught, they would be shot immediately. You got no second chance in this Nazi stronghold. I also learned that they had been teaching their children English in school since 1936. It was mandatory that they take at least one year. They were preparing in a big way for what they knew was coming, but what we at that time had little or no idea of. We were still sleeping, hoping that the Atlantic Ocean was broad enough to stave off any catastrophe.

Trolley time and now as before, it was quite crowded, however the guards decided that to wait any longer would be useless and dangerous, so we got aboard and started to camp. I was about to step on the platform when a man and woman came up to me with a small sleeping child in their arms. They held it out saying, "here you have not killed this baby yet, don't you want to do it now?" It was almost more than I could bear and felt like slugging the man right there, but one of the guards had been watching and immediately stepped up and pushed them back. They piled us into the front of the second car, thus leaving a partition between us and the civilians riding in the same car. A very good idea and one that no doubt saved lives, for the citizens of this "burg" Cherso, were really hostile toward airmen, and made no pretense of being otherwise. It seemed that they had the idea we killed babies just for the sport of it. It might be said right here and now that we did not intentionally kill babies, however, at times they probably were killed, because people were kept in dangerous areas and had not taken the proper precautions. From the height at which we bombed it was impossible to predict just who might be in the path of those bombs when they fell. If it happened that someone on the ground was foolish enough to be in such an area, rather than in a shelter, then he must take the consequences. Just how much consideration were they showing for the children in London and other large cities every time they loosed a "V bomb?" Absolutely none, for they were very unpredictable, even the Germans knew that. Often they turned around and killed the very men who started them on their way. When these bombs were released, all they particularly cared about was that they hit something. Whether it be a tenement house or factory, gave them little concern. But of course they claimed to know nothing about that, and probably didn't, so ill informed were they. Their minds had really been poisoned. Now that the war is over they shall have to be re-educated. What a job that is going to be!

Off the trolley and over to camp, which at this point was not visible. They told us it was one-half mile down the road. Whether it was or not, was a question. The injured men we had with us were having a difficult time keeping up, so we took turns carrying them by making slings with our arms. Either this or they would fall the victims of one or more of the vicious dogs that were bringing up the rear along with the guards.

We arrived at the tall entrance gates in about forty five minutes, and were herded over to the headquarters building of the barbed wire enclosure. Several of the guards entered the building, while the rest of them with their dogs, remained outside to keep us surrounded. It was freezing and the wind was blowing briskly from the north, all of which was doing an excellent job of chilling me to the core, for I had nothing on but my shirt and trousers. One goose pimple would move up to the other, and say "Get over boy, this is my spot." I felt like a poor grade of coarse sand paper, and was getting colder by the minute. Waiting an hour for the trolley had not helped matters any, but this was putting the finishing touches to what I thought sure would be a beautiful case of pneumonia. After standing another half hour I was finally called in by one of the guards. I walked up the steps and was led down the hall to the camp interrogator. I rapped once, opened the door, walked briskly in, giving him no indication that I was nearly frozen, saluted him, then remained standing at attention. He gave me at ease and told me to be seated, and relax. Well, I sat down all right, but whether or not I relaxed is debatable, for almost immediately he began firing questions at me.

"What is your name?"

This of course I gave him, and also my rank and serial number, and he began filling in the long form he had before him on his big impressive desk.

"What is your age?"

No answer.

"When were you shot down?"

No answer.

"To what group do you belong?"

Still all quiet.

"To what squadron did you belong?"

"Sir, I'm sorry, but I can give you no information other than my name, rank and serial number, and those you already have."

"What was your position on the ship?"

He went on just as though he had not even heard my previous statement.

"Where were you shot down?"

And so he went on and on, and of course all to no avail for I had made a decision and was going to stick to it.

"When is your birthday?"

"What are your parents' names?"

"What is their occupation?"

"What was your civilian occupation?"

"What year were you born?"

"To what church do you belong?"

"Where is the rest of your crew?"

Yes, I thought, wouldn't you like to know? That would indeed make you happy.

"How long is this war going to last?"

I had my ideas about that too, but this was definitely not the place to voice them. This fellow surely was persistent.

"Who is going to win this war?"

I would love to answer that, but still had better keep still. He was becoming acutely aware that to get any information from me was going to be next to an impossibility, and so I felt sure soon he would pass me by and try another victim. I knew that if they succeeded in getting even the slightest bit of information, other than name, rank and serial number they would just continue quizzing me, for that would be the cue for him that more would follow if he but had the patience. Once you weaken and give them just a little more than the required amount they really give you the "works." One thing just leads to another. Then the whole thing becomes a vicious circle. He gets all the desired information. You betray your buddies. That was not for me, they had me, but they would never get any of the other boys if I could help it.

"Well," he said "I guess you want to go back out in the cold again and wait 'til the last, maybe then you will talk."

To this I made no answer, but did plenty of thinking. I made up my mind that should worst come to worst, I would go back out, even though I dreaded the very thought of it. My goose pimples were still playing hide and seek with one another, each trying to out do the other in size.

"You are dismissed," he said.

So I arose, stood at attention, saluted him, did an about face and walked out. Assuming that I was to go back outside, for he had not retracted his statement, I headed for the outside door, only to be overtaken by a guard. He turned me around and led me up the hall until he came to the door of a cell. Remove your shoes, he commanded. I stooped over and did accordingly, after which I was admitted inside. I might have called it a cubicle, but I feel that would have been an overstatement for what greeted my eyes was far from encouraging. The cell was about four feet wide, and possibly eight feet long. It had a wooden bed, with a tow sack and one blanket. There was a small table in the corner with a dirty flask sitting on top. You can guess what I assumed the flask was used for but I fear your guess will be wrong. Mine was, I found out later that it was used to give the "guests" coffee with their meals. I took one look at the bed and decided it was too dirty to sleep in, but after sitting on the table for several hours I changed my mind and decided the dirt could be hanged for I would sleep in it anyway. Of course I was only kidding myself, for all the while I had been sitting on the table I had been slighting my "friends" and they aimed to get revenge. Now I had no more than hit the sack when the bugs, fleas and lice hit me with their sharpened mandibles and inside of a half-hour had me looking as though I had the measles. Needless to say I would rather have had the latter, but this was a case where likes and dislikes were not to be considered. A more horrible night I had never spent in my life – up to this time – but as I found out later this was just the beginning. The room was very cold, and of course this only served to make a bad situation worse, for it necessitated the use of the blanket. I can safely say the animals held the fibers together, but once I stretched it over me they forgot all about the fibers, and sat down to lunch. The room had an electric radiator in it, but they refused to turn it on. At first I failed to understand the reason for putting in heating devices if you were not going to use them, but upon quizzing other men who had gone through prior to me, I found that if you arrive in the summer when it is hot, then they will turn them on and make it even more uncomfortable and if you arrive in the winter, well, they will be real generous and let you freeze it out. It is a nice system and I should not be at all surprised that it brings results, with some of the men at least, for some people will do almost anything for comfort, others are so stubborn they refuse to yield under any circumstances, regardless of how trying. Yours truly belonged to the latter class and decided he would endure almost anything now for he had been thoroughly inoculated by everything that they army had, and last night by everything that the bed contained, and prior to that with all the cold the human body could absorb, so felt no desire to break down now. I was resolved to stick it out.

When morning finally rolled around, I squirmed out of that sack and shook myself off, but of course the "pets" that I had acquired refused to budge, so now I had company. Yes, very unpleasant company, and buddies for life, I was afraid. More mouths to feed if nothing else. I felt extremely dirty, for I had not been given a chance to wash since capture, so rang my buzzer. When the guard arrived I asked him in German, whether such facilities were available. He was so astonished that he had answered yes, almost before he realized what he was doing. He stepped out into the hall and directed me to where I might accomplish the feat. I knew that my newly acquired pets didn't exactly relish a clean body, and of course felt that this might be a way to get rid of some of them, but as I could not take a bath, I still harbored more than was comfortable. There being no soap available, the job was rather difficult for the dirt had worked deep down into the pores, but after several applications of water and lots of rubbing I did manage to remove the greater share of the filth. Anyway I did feel better even though there was still considerable evidence of "tattle tale gray" on my hands and face. My face was a mess anyway for it had crusted over, as a result of the burns received in the fire. If my mother would have seen her grown child in such a condition, she would in all probability have disowned him, and you couldn't rightly blame her, for there was a decided change in color.

I returned to my room, seated myself on the table and began looking around to see if I might spot any hidden microphones. The Germans had a nasty habit of sticking them around in all the rooms so they might listen to what you were saying. I failed to find any, but saw many places where one might easily have been secreted. I should not be at all surprised that such was the case either, for I had no more than begun to sing, when they called me back for another interrogation. Evidently sounded too happy. Right during my lunch hour too, so I hastily drank the coffee that had been poured into the filthy flask, and with sandwich in hand, strolled leisurely down the hall. Upon arrival I had eaten it, so was empty handed. I knocked once, entered very militarily, saluted and stood at attention.

"Just take that chair there," he told me, very warmly, so courteously in fact that I felt he must be ill. But wait, I was soon to find out the reason for all the unexpected hospitality. He was elaborately dressed and had Red Crosses sewed on his uniform as though he might be a Red Cross representative. Was he or was he not? That was the question. Frankly I doubted it for I could see no good reason for the Red Cross to come in a place like this and seek information. To make it even more convincing he had a new blank in front of him and this too had a beautiful Red Cross printed right on the top center. From all outside indications one would be led to believe he really represented the organization. But did he? His questions would soon give me the answer to that one, for I knew well enough that this organization would not be interested in where I was shot down or when, but what injuries I had received and what medical attention I had received, if any.

It certainly looked like the real "McCoy" all right, but once I began reading the questions, I knew what a prevaricator he was. Here are some of the questions.

What is your name? Your rank? Your serial number? So far so good. When were you born? With what group did you fly? How many missions have you flown? What are the names of your crew members? What became of them? What is your position on the ship? When were you shot down? Where do your parents live" What do they do for a living, etc.?

"What," I asked "does the Red Cross care about such information? Surely you don't expect me to be taken in by such a thing?

This he resented very much, and this was the final tip-off, for had he been on the level it would have disturbed him not at all. It confirmed the conclusions that I had drawn. It was truly fictitious and the "jig was up."

But did he give up? No, he had still another plan. He was going to salvage everything, by one last clever maneuver and take me in, so quick I would not know what happened. He hoped!

"Well, at least sign it on the bottom where it asks for your signature."

Sounded harmless enough, but it surely would have set him up beautifully. This would permit him to fill in the rest of the blank, with fictitious information. Then when a man came in, whom he thought to be from my crew, or even squadron, he would get it out of his desk and show it to him, signed and all, saying "well, Lt. Lienemann, did it, why can't you?" With a stroke of good fortune he could find out all about me and I'd never be the wiser as to where he had secured his information. Not knowing for sure whether he had any more schemes, and not desiring to take any further chances, I took the pencil and crossed out everything in every direction, so thoroughly that he could never attempt to erase it without tearing the paper. He told me to stop, so I immediately started all over and made it twice as bad. I then printed my name, rank and serial number in the spaces provided. This much information he could gladly have. Upon completion I handed it to him stating, "Sir, this is the best I can do under the circumstances." He was very angry, and his face had taken on renewed color, it was a delightful rosy red.

"Well," he said, "you will have to stay here until we get this information. You can go no further until this sheet is filled out."

I had heard that song before, so I wasn't unduly alarmed, as I had been the first time it happened.

"Sir, in that case you had better send me back to my cell, for as I see it I shall have to stay here with you for some time."

I always tried my best to be very courteous, and very military, in spite of how I felt, for it seemed I fared much better this way.

"You are dismissed," he said, his face again flushing, upon which I arose, gave him a salute, did an about face and walked out.

Once in the hall I ambled to my room but made no pretense about getting there in haste for I had drawn the conclusion that I might be a long time customer, so might just as well make myself a bit comfortable. Why hurry about getting from one place to the other. After all the more time I could spend meandering around the less time I would have to spend in the cell with my bunkmates, and the four blank walls. Quite frankly I didn't like those bloodsuckers, and didn't intend to give them anymore blood transfusions than was absolutely necessary. They could have made me much happier had they moved out and let me have the bed to myself for there just was not room for all of us anyway, secondly they had outworn their welcome already. Somehow they did not seem to mind their lot, for every day or at least the most every other day they got new blood. More aptly put, a fresh victim. I rather doubt if these bugs suffered any during the war, but all the boys who supplied them with "their daily blood" certainly were not too happy over the situation. The first look I took of that cell I decided it had not been thoroughly cleaned for four years, now I fear that was an underestimate. Upon return to my room I walked over to the window, and tried to get it open, but all to no avail, so planted myself again on the table. I would have much preferred to lie down for it is a more restful position, but rather than be nurse maid to the pets the bed contained, decided to sit it out. I had no more than gotten myself into a semi-comfortable position when the guard made his reappearance at the door. This was getting to be habitual. They wanted to see me again, and much the same ritual was forthcoming, but this one was shorter than ever. The more often they called me, the more determined I was they should secure no information. Surely they must have none, or they would not be so persistent. Anyway, it again provided me with the pleasure of leisurely walking up and down the hall. I made sure that I took plenty of time. At least a half hour would elapse before I returned to my room, even if I had to sneak off into the rest room, for a spell, and talk to whoever might come in. The guards were not too careful about watching me as I walked for there was no way to escape, other than the end doors, and men were posted there. Then too, there were never more than one or two men in the hall at the time, and this could quickly be determined by the guard in charge, by simply glancing down the hall, counting the doors swung out into it. If there were two, two men were out and no more could get out until either one or both of them had returned. In regard to number, they were very cautious, for apparently the fear of being overpowered lingered constantly in their minds, and should this happen every one would be set free.

After settling down in my cell for several hours, and making plans just what to do with myself for the following weeks, should the interrogator carry out his promise, which I honestly doubted, I was again startled by the rattle of keys at my door. This time the guard instructed me to fold up my blanket and put on my shoes which he threw to me. I was to be moved. Where to, how far, he didn't say. Perhaps to the dungeon where they put fellows who didn't talk. But I didn't worry about the situation for I knew full well that would do no good, but just decided to wait and see what was going to happen. Soon he began unlocking other doors, bringing other men out into the hall. When twenty had congregated, he sent us all down the hall to the exit. This brightened the picture considerably, but of course anything could still happen, nevertheless I had the satisfaction of knowing I would not be alone, regardless of what might turn up. How right I was, for we found ourselves marched out across the driveway, through the arch, which joined the headquarters building, and down the alley to several barbed wire enclosed detaining barracks. I learned from the boys, upon being admitted, that it was from this area I would be shipped to the next camp. O happy day, another interrogation over with, again they had proved themselves "liars." Soon I wouldn't believe anything they told me.

The barracks were huge and each room contained from thirty to forty double tier wooden bunks, with pets included, one dirtier than the next. But I could at least talk and jest with my fellow allies, so no longer had to look at the four blank walls. Lt. Chiles and I still had some unfinished business too, but this was no place to take it up, for the very walls had ears. Furthermore I had no intention of letting them discover that I knew him, for as yet we had not been through Stalag Luft and surely we were destined to go there unless they were no longer using the camp which seemed unlikely. At any rate we would not take that chance, but wait, for it seemed quite evident we would be shipping out together.

Night drew nigh and I had dinner. One slice of sour black bread with jam, and a cup of tea. The tea was so bitter that I poured it away. What its contents were I shall never know, but it was abominable to say the least. Upon completion, the guard entered and made us all remove our shoes, whereupon he tied them all in a bundle and left the room, locking the door behind him.

Bedtime, what a thought, ordinarily the best that could come to one's mind, but here it only meant another night of discomfort and agony. But in spite of the consequences I piled in, and had no more than struck the tow sack, when my little "buddies" came right out of their hiding places and went to work. Nursing time had drawn nigh. A nice quiet peaceful sleep, was not had by anyone, however the body was in a horizontal position so partial relaxation was in effect.

At the crack of dawn, I was awakened, and after considerable searching and scuffling, in the heap of shoes that had been thrown into the center of the room, I found mine, and put them on. Then I had my breakfast, a piece of sour black bread and jam, and fell out into the small yard, just in front of the barracks. We were lined up and counted off, to see that no one had disappeared. Satisfied that all were present the guard handed a list of names to the highest ranking American officer to read aloud. When he had finished he told us that those whose names had been called were to fall into a column of twos and proceed to the gate, from where we would march, under guard to the railroad station to again board the train. Destination, as heretofore, unknown, but everyone was of the same opinion, it was bound to be Stalag Luft for surely our arrival at that famous camp was overdue. Both Lt. Chiles and I had again made it and it appeared as though we were destined to be together, and for that we were both very happy. The ride was uneventful, and as usual without food or water. However, it lasted only eight hours, so I did not suffer to any appreciable extent. I had learned by this time that, regardless of how bad a situation was, it could always be worse, so just took things as they came, with no complaints. I knew only too well that many men who had not escaped with their lives, would gladly have traded places with me so dwelt on the good things, small as they were, and let it pass at that. It helped a great deal to make a really depressing situation somewhat bright, and I had to live with myself.

Upon arrival at Frankfurt we were removed from the train, lined up and counted, and then marched through the city to the triumphant jeers and ridicule of the German civilians, who lined the walks for the occasion. No doubt they thought they were winning the war, for how else could they have acquired such a large delegation of allied personnel, there being about 250 in our group. But what a small minute minority we represented of the whole that was facing them. Little did they know, far less did they care, it seemed, for they apparently were winning at the present. During the march, some of the men were stoned, while still others were shot by erratic civilians, but such is the lot of a prisoner. The rest of us had no choice, but to go on, thanking God that we had been spared such a horrible untimely death. Had they known then what we know now, they would probably never had been taken alive, but fought until the last drop of blood oozed from their veins, going down as heroes rather than martyrs to the cause.

Once out of the city we made our way up a winding cobblestone road, on either side of which were fields of rutabagas and potatoes. They were tempting indeed, but to get a bullet hole in exchange for a bite to eat, didn't seem very encouraging, so we left the vegetables alone. Then too, there were those ever present man eating police dogs, and I did not particularly care for a round with one, for I was sure to lose the battle. No, I would do without, until the chance was more inviting, and the inevitable results less costly.

Upon arrival at the gate the column was halted, and counted once more to see that no one had been spirited away. It was rather amusing to think that they would bother about counting us before permitting entry! I wonder what would have happened had we not all been there. Would we have had to wait outside of the high barbed wire fence until the missing members were found? Had that been the case, in another hour or so they most assuredly would have had their hands full, for by that time it would have been dark. Anything could have happened and probably would have. But, no one had managed to skip out, so he opened the gate, whereupon we entered and walked up to the headquarters building. That was it, Stalag Luft I, as I live and breathe. By single file we marched into the building all into a large room where we were seated, on the floor. Here I waited my turn to be called by the interrogator for another of those cross examinations. And I had not waited long before my name was called. I walked into his office, very militarily, saluted and stood at attention. He gave me at ease, which position I assumed without further hesitation.

First came the usual three questions, name, rank and serial number, but it had a different slant than previous encounters.

"My, that is a very good German name," he said, "you are fighting on the wrong side."

This of course brought a smile to my face, and I was not the least bit surprised that he recognized the name as such, everyone of them up to this time had done the same, but had never made such a statement. Never once was I questioned how to spell it either on quite this angle.

"Sir," I replied, "I might be fighting for the wrong side, but it appears to be the winning side."

"Oh, do you think so," he retorted.

"Yes, sir, such is my belief, and I don't think it will be too long before you too will see it that way."

With this he became a bit provoked, but went on asking me why and on what I based my opinion, but I refused to discuss this matter or any other matter any further for knew it would only draw me in deeper. I did not care to be involved at this point, for I had not at previous camps, so why jeopardize myself now. After a few minutes, he motioned for me to leave, so I assumed the position of attention, saluted him, did an about face, and walked out. The whole affair had not taken five minutes. He had my records from the previous camps before him, and no doubt noticed that they had failed too, so probably decided I was a hopeless case.

Once in the hall I was directed to a small room, with several tables. Here I was told to write a radiogram to my parents, or relatives. This they said would be read over one of the German broadcasting stations, and could be picked up by short wave in the States. I knew that they did read some of them over the air, for while still in England, I occasionally listened to their broadcasts.

Accordingly, I wrote the following message:

> Mr. and Mrs. A. H. Lienemann,
> Papillion, Nebraska
>
> "Am alive and well. Don't worry about me."
>
> Your son,
> Donald

I did give my parents' name and address by doing this, but actually it mattered little for once I got to prison camp they would take it from the letters addressed to them anyway. I had nothing to lose, so folded the message, handed it to the guard, and walked out in the direction he pointed, down the hall, and to my amazement the supply room. Here I was presented a Red Cross Prisoner of War Capture parcel. It was one of the finest surprises and highly treasured gifts that it has ever been my privilege to receive. What a Godsend, from thoughtful people in the United States! I opened it with the greatest of care and looked with glee at the items it contained. I doubt if a child could have been any happier upon finding a stocking, brim full, in front of the fireplace on Christmas morning. What this parcel meant to me in dollars and cents is impossible to say, for the figure has not yet been determined.

Its contents were all essentials that I was badly in need of, for I had only the clothing in which I was standing. To the best of my knowledge this is a complete list of the contents, any omissions are entirely accidental:

2 large bath towels

1 pair pants (olive drab)

1 shirt (olive drab)

1 necktie

2 pair summer underwear

2 suit winter underwear

1 wool knit sweater

5 pair socks

1 pair pajamas

1 pair house slippers

2 pair shoestrings

5 handkerchiefs

20 razor blades

1 comb and 3 bars hand soap

2 bars laundry soap

1 toothbrush

1 can toothpowder

1 carton gum

8 oz. chocolate

1 tube shaving soap

5 packages of cigarettes

2 rolls toilet tissue

1 capture card (to be sent home)

1 packet 1" adhesive compresses

The capture card indicated receipt of the parcel, and also told my folks that I was alive and well, I was also issued an army coat, 1917 vintage and blouse. This material was all sent in by the American Red Cross, and was given out by the allies who the Germans had working in the supply department. Those boys who came through with their coats, were not issued another, only those of us who had had ours taken away from us. It depends entirely upon who captures you, what clothing is taken away. I can say that my captors did a fine job of stripping me down to the bare essentials, and that I have frozen royally as a result. What the outcome would be I did not know. I could only hope the relief received here would stave off a catastrophe.

Having received my full allotment I was directed back to the road in front of headquarters. Here I waited until twenty men had assembled and then marched off to the main compound. Once inside its portly gates we were taken directly to the showers. Pleasant surprise number 2, and almost more than I could stand in such short order. The allies were in charge of the bathing and took every precaution to see that we were properly deloused, if we had any lice, which nearly everyone did. After washing with kerosene, I entered the shower, and had a nice hot bath. The hot water ran for four minutes, the limit set by the Germans, and was then turned off. This was indeed short, especially for such a dirty body, but I was very happy to have gotten this much. It was great to be partially clean anyway. I put on clean clothes, and was taken to my barracks. The barracks were much cleaner than any of the others encountered thus far, and this was largely due to the untiring efforts of the American officer the Germans had put in charge of the billeting and cleanliness. He had full jurisdiction over the prisoners once they entered the compound, and made each responsible for cleaning up his area, which needless to say we were all very glad to do. The barracks were divided into rooms, each room housing more than forty men. The bunks were four tiers high, with tow sack for mattress, and had one blanket. Not much, but better than sleeping outside. I made my bed, then chatted a bit with the other men in the room, after which I fell out for "chow." The food was prepared and served by the Americans, and consisted of food sent in by the American Red Cross in their Prisoner of War Food parcels. The first American food since that fatal day and right in the heart of Germany. I must be dreaming, but no, it was real, no two ways about it. The parcels contained the following articles, with occasional variations:

    1 lb. powdered milk

    1 lb. margarine

    6 oz. Pate

12 oz. Spam

12 oz. Corned Beef

18 oz. Salmon (or sardines)

7 oz. C Ration Biscuit

8 oz. Sugar

8 oz. Cheese

15 oz. Prunes (or raisins)

6 oz. Jam

2 oz. Concentrated Coffee

8 oz. D. Bar Chocolate

7 Ascorbic Acid Tablets

5 Packages Cigarettes

2 Bars soap

2 Packages Salt and Pepper Mixture (we never saw them except in rare instances when we slipped one out)

A finer selection could not have been made for they were very satisfying, especially to hungry men, and we were most definitely in that category. I stopped in the small hallway on my way out of the mess hall, to mail the capture card I had filled out and addressed, then returned to the barracks, to see if I could find Lt. Chiles. After considerable searching I finally located him, but as it was too cold and dark to go outside, we decided to postpone our talk until morning. Early the next morning I arose, took my dirty clothes to the hydrant, and washed them thoroughly with soap and water. This I was quite sure the best way to get rid of the pets they still contained, for as I remembered biology they did not like anything clean. I then tacked them to the south of the barracks and went to breakfast, after which I immediately sought out Lt. Chiles. I finally found him and so we sat down on the grass to continue where we had left off. Neither of us had heard anything further about Sgt. Damrel the engineer who had bailed out, but had not been seen since. Nor could we find any trace of him from other men who had gone down the same day. He seemed to have disappeared in thin air, if such a thing were possible. Lt. Chiles knew nothing more of any of the still unaccounted for crewmembers, so I related to him just what I knew of their fate. I distinctly remember seeing three men go whizzing by, when I opened my chute, and fell into the forest. These men I knew must have been from our ship and were freed from its flaming clutches, at the same time I was, and by the same force. There was one big difference, they never regained consciousness and could not open their chutes. These men I believed to be Lt. McGuinness, the bombardier, Sgt. Rattin, the waistgunner and Sgt. Gurman, the radio gunner. The latter's fate we had already, so that left but the first two to give further consideration. Lt. McGuinness I was sure went whizzing by as I opened my chute, and fell unconscious into the forest, the fall killing him instantly. My reason for thinking this, was the fact that we were both in the nose, and were undoubtedly both hurled from it at the same time, and in the same direction. Just where or how shall forever remain a secret, for I remember nothing but the very instant of the explosion. This being the case, we would have fallen nearly side by side until I regained consciousness and opened my chute. I know there was a man near me when I opened it and this I am sure must have been Lt. McGuinness, a tall naturally curly haired blonde from New York City. What a bombardier he was! He gave the Germans plenty to think about while he was in the business.

Sgt. Rattin, and Sgt. Gurman I feel sure were released at the same time, for they were standing the same place in the plane evidently, side by side, for one was handling the right waist gun, and the other the left. Sgt. Gurman had been found and his dog tags reported to Lt. Chiles, but no mention was made of Sgt. Rattin. I know they did not fall in the same spot. However, there could not have been more than thirty of forty feet between them, or at last so it appeared when I witnessed them, but of course this was only for a split second, so I might easily have been mistaken. Had I taken the time to hunt these bodies, when I parachuted into the forest some fifteen seconds later, I would have known the answer. But I also knew that if I did take that time I would surely be captured and that I did not want to happen. Had it been a case of helping injured men I would have searched for them and taken the chance of getting caught, but I was certain they had not fallen 26,000 feet and lived. It just was not humanly possible.

From all appearances, an excellent waist gunner too was lost forever to the world. A tragic end for such a fine young man who was always anxious to help others. This left us with little hope, and only one man yet undiscussed, Sgt. Fischer, the tail gunner. All the attacks had come from the rear, and we knew that a good many 20 mm's had hit the area. Just how badly he was wounded, neither of us knew for the interphone was out, thus contact with him after the battle started was out of the question. The tail, without a doubt, was blown off, as a result of the explosion, and this left us with the faint thread of hope that it might have glided to the earth, and he had been discovered and taken to the hospital. If that had not happened, the handwriting was on the wall, for it would mean of the seven that were in the ship at the time of the explosion, only I had lived to tell the tale. It seemed unbelievable that such should be the case, but when I thought of how close I actually came to meeting the same fate, it was not too hard to believe. It was nothing short of miraculous and the deeper I went into the thing, the more amazing it became. Why, I kept asking myself should I be spared, when apparently all the rest were taken? That question stumped me, and try as I may I could find no answer to it, so let it go. What else was there to do until I could be certain of everyone's fate! This then closed our session for the time, and we both made our way back to our respective rooms.

During the afternoon we were called from the barracks, lined up and counted off. Immediate destination, Frankfurt Railroad Station. Ultimate destination our permanent prison camp, wherever that might be. If we go to the same camp the previous shipment has gone, it will be Stalag Luft 1, Barth Germany, if not, only the Germans know. This left us pretty much in the dark, as was the usual procedure, but it puzzled us very little as we walked to the station, for sooner or later we were bound to arrive somewhere. Lt. Chiles was with the group too so we would surely end up in the same camp, unless something separated us on the way, and it did not seem likely.

Chapter VI
Dangerous Journey

Upon arrival at the station, we were all given one complete Red Cross Prisoner of War Food Parcel and boarded the train immediately thereafter. All indications pointed to the fact that it will be a long trip. They cautioned us that this would have to last us until arrival, regardless of how long it might take. Consequently I took it very easy on my rations, for I had no desire to do without, should the trip last too long.

Into each compartment of the train, which accommodated six, ten were quite cozy, so cozy in fact that if all ten entered, the door to the small aisle could not be closed. This compartment then would be our home until arrival at the permanent prison camp. How many days hence that might be, was entirely a matter of personal conjecture, the guesses all the way from 2 to 7 days. We all hoped that it would not be the latter, more than that we were powerless to do. If it should prove to be Barth, Germany, we would have a long way to go, for now we were in southern Germany, near the Rhine River, and as I remembered Barth, it was somewhere north of Berlin, however, I was not at all sure. I remember it being mentioned once during a briefing, which was to take us to Berlin. We flew the northern route that day, so it must of necessity lie north of that city. Had I known then what I know now, I would have taken closer notice, and memorized its location, but as it was I left it slip haphazardly, for after all it was just another city to be flown over. Even now we were not at all sure we were going there so why worry about it.

The time had arrived to come to some sort of an agreement how we were going to ride in our crowded compartment. At first it seemed an impossibility to manage under any arrangement, but the more we thought about it, the more ideas we got. After considerable discussion, pro and con, it was decided that one man would be sleeping all the time on our makeshift bed. The bed being the luggage rack near the ceiling of the train. This meant a little less than 2 1/2 hours per man, for we planned to share it equally amongst the ten of us. Six men could sit fairly comfortably in the compartment. So we had seven taken care of, but that still left three men to dispose of in one manner or the other. What should be done with them? We could not send them to another compartment, for everyone had the same problem. After further consideration, it was decided to put the three largest men on one side, and then maybe four of the smaller ones could take up the other seat. It worked so another had been placed, but that was the end. The fates of the two remaining men were now at stake. It had to be the small aisle or nothing. It meant standing during the day and lying down at night, if you could find the space. This then was to be our arrangement for the duration of the trip, and we would exchange with one another as we went along thus giving every man a fair share of rest and relaxation. It would be little enough as it was.

Dusk, and still we had not moved from the spot where we loaded. It seemed an eternity, but actually only a couple of hours had elapsed. I began to wonder if there had been some mistake when the car gave a lurch. An engine had backed down the siding and hooked on. Soon we would be on our way. There were three cars of prisoners and each car had a white P.O.W. painted on the top of it for identification. The windows were covered with a network of bars welded to the car itself. Had they used bolts, to secure them, we might have tried getting them loose, but to break a weld, that was another matter entirely. There was no rear door to the car and the front one was kept locked at all times. We were really cooped in. But it still did not prevent us from looking for other ways to escape.

Another lurch, another jerk, and we were under way, part of a regular passenger train making its way east. This was of short duration though for we had not traveled more than three hours, when we were attached to a freight train. Progress was slow, but we were moving, and that was the most important issue at the time. I doubt if we missed a siding or a small town en-route. Whatever our destination might be they certainly were in no hurry to get us there. This slow aggravating rate continued until nine in the morning and then we found ourselves parked right in the heart of a large railroad marshaling yard. What a beautiful location – and completely surrounded with ammunition cars, troop trains, switch engines and everything else that had any value. Just exactly the kind of a setup any bomber group would love to hit, and precisely what fighter squadrons go out to attack every day. A more inviting set up I have never seen, and to top it off the sky was crystal clear. Surely they would not leave us here, like a bunch of ducks in a pond, to be the victims of the first allied planes that fly over. But try as I may to convince myself otherwise, that seemed to be the case. There was no getting around it, and there was no means of escape, for the cars had been locked. What to do, was the question. But where was the answer? For the moment it was not forthcoming. I listened intently. Wasn't that the hum of engines? Or was I just hearing things? I asked some of the others to listen too. Yes, it was, but it was still quite faint. I searched the western sky through a slit in the top of the window, but could see nothing. The hum increased, there was no longer any doubt. They were getting closer. Would this be the target? Oh God, please forbid, for we have not a ghost of a chance. The men were uttering silent prayers in their own behalf, as well as for the entire group. The hum had increased to a drone, and the sirens of the city were shrieking their warning.

Civilians were scurrying breathlessly to the air raid shelters. But we sat tight knowing full well what would happen should they decide to drop the deadly missiles here. I could see them now, off in the distant horizon, in wing formation, coming ever onward. It looks like "Forts," shouted one of the boys, and in another few minutes, they were definitely identified as such. Fortresses had a nasty habit of hitting marshalling yards too, which we knew only too well, for it was not but about a week ago, I was doing the same thing. This thought gave me no comfort whatsoever, but worry would help none at all. Praying was the only answer, and that I lost no time in doing. But there was no stopping them. The only remaining hope was that they had a different target for today, than the one in which we were situated. Time was the all-important element and in a matter of minutes the answer would be known. They continued on, the drone had increased in intensity until it almost reached a roar. There were hundreds of them. The guards, who had been watching the train, went to the shelter, to let us sweat out our fate by ourselves. We were going nowhere they knew, for we were securely locked in. For the first time in my life I had the feel of what it meant to be on the receiving end of those horrible bombs. I did not like it, I didn't like it a bit, but the thing I hated most was the fact that we were not even given a rat's chance. At least I had been that fair, but this was no time to quibble. The roar of the engines drew closer, and my breathing became more difficult. My heart began to pound, no longer taking those rhythmic pulsating beats. It seemed this would be it for they were heading straight in our direction. Sometimes I believe this would have pleased the Germans very much, even though they would have lost some valuable equipment. At any rate they were going to be very sure that we were hit if anything was dropped for they had us stacked right in the midst of everything where the chances of a complete miss were so meager, they were not worth mentioning. The bombers had nearly reached us by this time, and were still in wing formation so I breathed easier. It seemed unlikely that they would bomb us in that type formation, for the practice generally followed called for a breakup into groups. This they had not done, and so they were in all probability going on by to another target. This to the tune of great rejoicing amongst the prisoners, and many silent prayers of thanks for deliverance in this our hour of need. Moments like that certainly strengthen one's faith in a Divine Being, and make him very sure that there is a God above who does protect His loved ones, if He deems it wise.

The all clear soon sounded, and the guards made their reappearance. They did not say anything, but their expressions told volumes. Not alone had they deliberately jeopardized our very lives, but they were gloating over their achievement. It would have been entirely unnecessary to park us there in the first place, for there were plenty out of the way sidings outside of the city proper where we would have bothered no one, and the risk would have been nil. They knew the hours of daylight raids were between nine and three, and if one should come they were going to be very sure we were on the receiving end. At least such is my honest opinion, and I know it is shared by thousands of others who had a taste of the same thing. It was a hair raising experience that I never care to repeat, but my mind was soon removed from that channel of thinking for the train gave a start, a jerk, and down the tracks we rolled. Now I thought, surely we will continue uninterrupted until we arrive at our destination.

While walking down the aisle, I noticed one of the men had on a nice new pair of GI shoes. Inquisitive as to where he acquired them, I stopped and asked. "Why the Germans gave me these."

"The Germans gave them to you, now pray tell where would they get them?"

"They told me that they had been taken from an American they found dead in the forest."

"Did they give you any details, as to the day they were found, or on whom?"

"They gave them to me the day I was shot down, and that was the 11th. You see, I was not wearing my shoes at the time, only my heated felt boots. I had difficulty walking in them so they, the Germans, gave me the shoes."

"Do you recall anything special about how they were fastened together?"

"Say, you are getting pretty inquisitive, aren't you?"

"That I shall be forced to admit I am, and for a very good reason, You see, I am quite certain my bombardier was killed that same day, however, there is a very slim chance that he may not have been. It is that slim chance I am trying to track down, so when I do finally get home I will know definitely one way or the other and can tell his parents."

"In that case I shall be only too glad to tell you, and I am very sorry for seeming rude."

"That is perfectly okay, you had a right to know."

"They were fastened together with a piece of wire, making two hoops about eight or ten inches in diameter."

"So far it fits perfectly, go on. How about the knot, do you remember anything in particular about it?"

This I especially wanted to know, for I had helped Lt. McGuinness at the time he wired his shoes together and knew just how it was tied, for I had done it. He never wore his shoes either, but always attached the wire hoop to one of the snaps on his parachute harness. Thus he would never leave without his shores, and when he opened his chute, should the necessity arise, he need have no fear of losing them, due to the terrific change in momentum. If you secured them by the shoestrings, they would snap off, and you would find yourself without shoes upon arrival on the ground, which needless to say, many boys did.

"To begin with," he said, "one hoop was through the eyes of one shoe, the other hoop through the eyes of the other. I know for certain that there were small eyelets made on the ends of the wire for I had a hard time getting the wire through the eyes. One of the guards finally became impatient, and cut one end off, so I might get it done quicker."

"That is what I have been waiting to hear. I most definitely do not like the news, but I would rather know for sure than labor under false illusions. You, my friend, have Lt. McGuinness' shoes. There is no mistake about it. I am very glad to see you walking in them, but at the same time I would much rather have seen the owner himself wearing them, and you still in your felt boots, for then there would have been another in our midst."

"Yes," he said, "I can see your point, and quite honestly I would only be too happy to give them up if such an arrangement could be made, but as we both know that can never be done now."

"Truer words were never spoken," and with that I departed.

I went back to my compartment and ate supper. I ate from my faithful Red Cross box, so did quite well, and have no complaints to offer. It was not like home, but it was far better than sour black bread.

All night we poked along, stopping at every hamlet, only to find ourselves in the same predicament the following morning when nine o'clock rolled around. Right in the center of the largest marshaling yard they could find, and just as before they were busy surrounding us with everything of value, explosives and otherwise. The very thing that I had dreaded, and hoped never to go through again. They loved us, yes they did, just like so much dirt under their shoes, and were doing everything possible to have us rubbed out by our own men prior to arriving at prison camp. This sort of thing was definitely not in accordance with the Geneva Convention regulations, and if any one can show me that it is, I will gladly eat the articles one by one, but at this moment I was in no position to make my feelings understood, least of all carried out.

I had but one alternative, and that was to pray, and that I did to the best of my ability. Come eleven o'clock, the bombers were on their way. They continued on, we continued to pray, but they kept coming. Once we had missed, would we be that lucky again? This just could not go on forever, for sooner or later the law of averages was bound to catch up with us. Not today though for again they flew over the top, and on to their briefed target. I knelt and thanked God that He had again seen fit to spare me. Twice it seemed to me was about all that such a thing could happen to anyone and now that we were further from the Rhine surely it would not occur again. With this thought in mind I was somewhat relieved, and with the train again in motion I had other things to think about.

A guard had entered the car, and was slowly walking down the aisle, checking each of the compartments as he came. When he came to our compartment, I started visiting with him, for I spoke some German, and this pleased him very much. After he had completed his checking he returned, and I stepped out into the aisle to see what information I might be able to wheedle out of him. I was very much interested in seeing if I might find out just where we were going so approached him on the subject. First, he was rather hesitant about telling me, but later said that to the best of his knowledge we were going to Barth, and that it would take about four or five days, depending entirely on how much we stopped or were delayed enroute. At least I knew that much, however, there was always the chance that he might be misleading me, but I rather doubted it, for he further told me that he was going to try to get a pass after arrival to go to see his family. He lived about fifty miles from there, and showed me the photo of his wife, and three children, as well as a picture of his home. To top it off with, and this surprised me no end, he said that at the cessation of hostilities, I should stop in and have a glass of wine with him. Apparently he had no ill feelings toward us, if so he gave no such indication. He did not say who was going to win the war to make that wine drinking possible, and I did not quiz him about it, either, for I had no desire to arouse ill feelings in him towards me. He might be an invaluable aid during the remainder of this trip, and as long as I had to give him no information, but could satisfy him, just by visiting, I had nothing to lose. This, I thought was a real opportunity to get the answer to a question I had been wondering about for a long time. I had wondered about it when I first heard it in the States years ago, but never once thought I would find myself in a position to obtain the information first hand. This was it, either he would answer it, or he would not. Personally I had nothing to lose either way.

"Is it true," I asked him, "that Frauleins were gathered together and placed in camps there to mingle with soldiers who were run in with them?"

A startling question to ask anyone, least of all the enemy, but I wanted to know the truth about the matter, and this was the only way I could figure out to get it. First he hesitated, then later frankly admitted that it had taken place, the chief purpose was to get more babies for "Der Fuehrer," preferably boys. He further admitted that at one time he had been sent into one of these camps. There was the clear unvarnished truth, from the mouth of one who had taken part. That was enough for me so I dropped the subject right there and bade him goodbye, telling him I would see him again tomorrow if he came through the car.

I slept in the aisle during the night and woke up the next morning with a stiff neck, and lame back. But these ailments got little attention, for come nine thirty, we were again parked in a railroad marshaling yard. This was just too much and I was at the point of explosion, but what good would it have done? None, absolutely none. It might have pleased the Germans to know they were getting my goat, and by heck they were not going to get that much satisfaction.

Noon came, and another raid was on, just as the two previous days, but again they went on by and left us undisturbed. The law of averages was certainly in our favor but how much longer it could last under the present strain was hard to determine. It seemed the scale had bent over backwards in our direction and it was about time that it went the other way. Needless to say we all prayed fervently that such a thing would not happen, and that we would be spared the ugly death the Germans were doing their level best to make us a part of.

But as the night passed, and the following day drew near, we knew our wish was not to be. No sir, we had not been frightened enough. They left us parked in the main marshaling yards of Stettin. I could think of a dozen reasons for bombing this area. It had a high priority on our bombing list, being a Baltic seaport, with direct rail service to Berlin, just some 60 or more miles away. The only satisfaction I had was that we must be somewhere within the vicinity of our prison camp, but what good would it do if I never got there. The point was to arrive alive, and in a walking state, not in a bundle or wooden box. However, I had survived three such hectic days with the aid of the good and gracious Lord and surely He would not let me down now. The noon hour passed, the raid went by, and we were spared once more. I doubt if more favoritism had ever been shown to a group of men by the Lord, and we thanked Him most graciously for His protection.

Perhaps, dear reader, by this time you are wondering why the bombers drop their loads on railroad yards when there are prisoners of war in cars in them. This is quite easily explained in this manner. It is an impossibility to determine what is in a car from the altitude at which bombers are forced to fly, due to safety reasons. You just cannot tell from five miles up, what is in them, and you could never read the small P.O.W. painted on their tops in white, unless you had a high powered glass. You can see the cars, but there is no way to tell a passenger or troop train, from those carrying prisoners. Even if it were possible I doubt very seriously whether the bombs would be carried on for when a target is once selected it is given such a high priority, that everything else is sacrificed to get it. What you go after today, may not be there tomorrow, so it must be today or never in many cases.

Shortly after the raid we started for Barth and upon arrival there parked on a small siding just outside of town. This brought to a close one of the most nerve wracking trips that I have ever made by train, and I certainly never want to go through anything like it again as long as I live. I know that I lost plenty of sleep and was tired beyond all hope of recovery, but sweating out these raids surely did not help matters any, neither did it increase my love for the Germans who locked up the car, and ran to the air raid shelter like a bunch of cowards. The least they could have done was to have left it open thus permitting us to disperse should a raid have taken place. As it happened it was not necessary, but came plenty close to being. I shall be forced to admit that we were very fortunate and that the Lord never once forgot us during the entire trip, but I might say in the same breath that many of the boys that went before and after me did not fare so well. A good many thousand died as a result of being put into such precarious positions by the enemy. The sad part of it is that those same fellows are not with me today to tell the story. They died a truly heroic death, with not even a rat's chance for survival. Mere martyrs to the cause.

We were still locked in the car and with nothing further to draw my attention, my mind began to ramble over all that had actually occurred during that hazardous trip just completed. I noticed particularly that nearly every industrial city, through which we passed, there was little left other than a mass of wreck and ruin. What formerly had been growing, thriving, buzzing factories were now hulks of ghost like buildings, with nothing but burnt out interiors and heaps of rubble. Many homes in the immediate areas had suffered a similar fate and were now shambles of their former selves. They had been laid to waste by the overwhelming power of Allied air bombardments.

Then there were the railroads and roads in Germany. The roadbed of the former was laid with all steel ties on a two foot thickness of crushed rock with no weeds or trash evident on either side. Never need they remove rotten or burnt out ties, as is so often the case in the United States. As for the roads, well they were either four or six lane affairs with a beautiful green, well plotted strip down the center. They skirted all the towns and villages and permitted vehicles to move on them at an unlimited speed so gradual were the curves.

Still another thing that had not exactly escaped my attention was the cleanliness and immaculately dressed Germans that we saw in nearly every station through which we passed.

Girls were dressed in silk dresses, fur coats, and silk hose, with beautiful hair dos and plenty of make up to go with it. They seemed to have suffered none of the ravages of war that one would have supposed they would. Not even in the line of food, for from all appearances they were well fed. There was not a sickly or starved looking one in the entire lot.

But the most distressing of all the things I saw and probably the most enduring, was the shameful use to which they were putting Red Cross cars. I saw them loaded with troops, shells, gasoline and everything else imaginable, heading for the front. These trains they had carelessly pulled up along side of us while stationed in the railroad yards, along with others, while sweating out the air raids. In this regard I shall leave you to draw your own conclusions for I have already drawn mine.

Upon arrival of additional guards from prison camp, my trend of thought was interrupted, for we got off the train, lined up in a column of five and were counted off.

Chapter VII
Prison Camp

Satisfied that we were all there they marched us off to the camp, which at this time was not visible. We were all looking anxiously in every direction for some trace of it, when finally one of the boys spotted one of the guard towers. All eyes were cast in that direction. That was it. Sure enough. Our home until the war was over, or until we managed some way to elude our captors. We had drawn much nearer by this time, and could hear the dogs barking, as if in eager anticipation of some new meat in which to sink their fangs. The gates were swung wide, and we marched direct to headquarters, where we were again lined up and counted off. We were then called inside, one at a time for a final interrogation. The interrogators, all high ranking men, were very insistent that they get the still missing information from us. When called I entered the room very militarily as before and stood in front of the desk at attention. He told me to be seated, and I did just that for I was utterly fatigued. After taking a look at my records, which had preceded me, he looked at me and said.

"Lieutenant, you might just as well talk here, for it won't make any difference anyway." "You see I have no way to get the information back to the German High Command so you can do no harm to yourself or your buddies."

Now wasn't that ducky? Just how stupid did he think I was? Did he really believe in his own mind that he could convince me of that? If it would not do the German High Command any good, why did he want to know? What was his particular interest? Surely it could not help him personally! On second thought it could have done him an immeasurable amount of good, for had he succeeded he would have accomplished something that none of the others had thus far. What a feather in his cap that would have been!

"Sir, I am very sorry, but I can give you no additional information."

"You can at least tell me when your birthday is, for surely that won't harm anything."

Perhaps not I thought, but if I tell you that, then you will only want to know more. I had no desire to be dragged into anything.

"Sir, I cannot answer that question."

This did not please him any too well, for he had failed. He knew in his own mind that I was doing the right thing, but of course to admit it would only be incriminating himself, and that he could never do in my presence. At least it would not be very advisable to do such, for the penalty he might have to pay as a result would be tragic. But he still had not given up.

"I will personally see to it that you get some additional clothes if you give me some of this information."

"Sir I can not give you any further information under any conditions whatsoever."

Hearing this he wrote something on my interrogation sheet under the title "Comments," gave me my P.O.W. number, which was "5564," sent me into an adjoining room for a final shakedown. I saluted him, did an about face and walked out. I could not help but wonder what he had written on the paper, under comments, for I had told him nothing. Perhaps sometime later I would learn the answer. I walked down the hall a few doors and stepped into the room indicated by the guard. The searchers soon relieved me of my clothes and capture kit, and were busy making a thorough search of it. They were going to be very sure that I did not succeed in smuggling anything into the camp itself that might have been missed by some previous "inspections." Every place that I had been interrogated I had been searched too, but from the very beginning they missed one compass, and as luck would have it they still had not found it anywhere along the way. Would my luck hold out, or was I to lose it now? Actually I did not need it, and would probably not have any occasion to use it in the future, nevertheless, it would give me a lot of satisfaction just to know that I had been able to hide one thing from those haughty "supermen." They carefully searched one garment after the other, inspecting seams and double portions with meticulous care, while I kept holding my breath for fear that they might locate it. I could not be at all sure just what the next move might be should they discover something at this stage. They might throw me back into solitary for concealing it, but I did not worry unduly about that for should the turn of events bring such a thing about, it could be endured. Not much use in jumping at hasty conclusions for they had not found the compass in four previous searches, so I should stand a good chance now. The law of averages said it was about time that I was losing it, but perhaps the law was not in effect. At least I hoped not! I gave a quick look in their direction and noticed they had just laid down the article containing it! Spared! My luck was still with me, and I as much as had it in camp.

I dressed and was sent to the central shower room and there again examined for lice, ticks, fleas, etc. by the American and British in charge of disinfection and sanitation, of the camp. After thoroughly washing with kerosene, I took a steaming hot shower. This treatment must have done the trick, for I don't remember being bothered by a single flea, bedbug, or louse again. While showering they had put my clothes under pressurized live steam and killed any bugs they might have been harboring in them, so now I was thoroughly clean and ready to go into the assigned compound. First, however, I had to go to the clothing store operated by Americans, and again issued clothes sent in by the American Red Cross. I acquired a cap, which I had been without up to this time. As I walked out the door I was confronted by two burly Germans, who had large opened jack knives in their hands. What I wondered, had I done now. Surely they were not going to slit my throat right here. Nope, they just wanted to cut the buttons off my overcoat, so that I could no longer button it.

"Why, I asked, are you doing this?"

"So you can not escape so easily," the one replied.

"Are you kidding," I asked, feeling sure they must be pulling my leg.

"Those were the instructions we were given."

It sounded pretty silly to me, but perhaps that was the case. You could make no sense out of what these fellows did anyway half of the time. I did know that if I ever had the slightest intention of escaping, those buttons would be the least of my worries, for I would sew on wooden ones, or some fashioned from tin. I rather think they needed a few buttons for the German army, and they were of the opinion that we could do without them much easier than their army in the field. However, I could be wrong.

Without any further ado, we were assembled into groups of twenty and started on the trek to our compound, which was North "II". This necessitated going by the South Compound and North I. As we passed by, all the old "Kreigies" ran to the fence and crowded up against it to see if they could recognize anyone in our group. If they did so, they would shout out the name of the individual. Thus old friendships were reestablished. But the one thing above all that they wanted to know, was "when will the war be over?" Frankly, I doubted if it would last until Christmas at the rate the armies were traveling and told them so. However, I could not be at all sure that they would continue the pace they were now making. Better said, were making when I last had contact with them, and that was nearly two weeks ago. What had happened since then I had not the slightest idea. Only time would tell. Upon reaching the outside gates of North II Compound we halted, and despite trouble with the keys the gate was finally opened, and we entered the forelager, only to be stopped once more. This time to be counted before entrance into the main compound itself. Having satisfied himself that there were twenty in the group, he opened the main gate to let us in. The prisoners who were already in the compound had formed a long winding trail, by lining up on either side making an aisle down which we walked. This made identification very easy for the boys already in camp, for they had a chance to see everyone of us as we came down the aisle. I was surprised beyond all measure to find that three of my navigation classmates were here, and all three of them in the reception line to boot. Almost like homecoming, but under drastically different circumstances. I chatted with the boys for awhile, gave them the latest news to which I had access, and then went on to the American Commanding Officers Headquarters located in block seven, room 9, as instructed. Upon entering the room I was introduced to Col. Spicer, the allied C.O. as were the others who followed.

"Laddies," he said, "let me welcome you to your new home." "It is not like the one you left some time ago, and you will find many things very inconvenient, but remember – many of your fellow men were not as fortunate as you." "You will be called upon to endure many hardships heretofore unknown to you, but take them in your stride and you will be the better men for having made the best of a rather regrettable situation. In this compound we have very few rules, but those we do have I ask you to follow. Let me list just a few of them to you as they come to my mind."

"First, there is what is commonly known as the "guard system," better known to all prisoners as "go on guard." It consists of having a man stationed at each entrance to your barracks all hours during which the doors are unlocked, and that is from six or six-thirty in the morning until eight at night, at which time the barracks are again barred. The guard's duty is to warn the rest of the men in the barracks every time a German approaches the door, thus if they have anything they do not want him to find they have a reasonable length of time to hide it, instead of being caught completely unaware, which would otherwise be the case. You can use any system you like in selecting the men for the jobs, but try to divide it evenly amongst the whole barracks and that way it will not work a hardship on anyone. I think that will about suffice for the guard system. Its chief purpose as you can readily ascertain is to aid us in keeping track of the Germans, so as not to be caught red handed doing something we know they would not condone."

The area in which you find yourself locked up in is not too big, as you no doubt have already noticed, but I do urge you all to take a little exercise each day, if possible, to keep in some semblance of condition. Remember your health is important. Medical attention is at a premium, for we have but three doctors and a dentist to care for all 10,000 of you. Don't forget, the buildings might be wired for something other than electricity. Never talk about anything military after lockup. The Germans crawl under the barracks and listen to your conversation. If they don't know who you are or anything about you, don't be foolish and tell them now. Play the game safe and keep your mouth shut; however, if you must talk go out to the center of the area where you are sure you can not be overheard and do it there. There will be roll call twice a day. The morning count is usually taken at seven, and the evening at five thirty, but both are subject to change, without notice, at the discretion of the detaining power. In other words, when the bugle blows prepare to fall out. If I had my way Laddies, there would be no roll call, but I am given my orders by the German over me, so have no alternative, but to carry them out." "In each of your barracks", he went on, "you will find a man that I have chosen to be your immediate commanding officer, and to him you will be responsible. If at any time anything disturbs you, ask him to help you, I am sure he will only be too glad to do so. Now then, as to mail. You are permitted, by the Geneva Convention Regulations to write three letters and four cards per month if you are an officer, and I notice everyone in this group is. These must be written on the forms provided by the Germans for this purpose, and must be lettered in ordinary pencil. If you use either ink or indelible pencil they will be destroyed. I can not guarantee you that the letters will ever arrive, but I do urge you to write to your parents or wives. Then at least you have discharged your obligation. Be very careful what you write though, for remember the Germans read them too. If they don't know anything about you, don't enlighten them."

He further told us that it would be necessary to be identified by someone already in camp. "This is very necessary," he said, "for all I know you might easily be a German spy dressed in an American uniform. Some of them speak fluent English too, you know, for they have been to the States and returned, just to aid Germany in such a cause. We have found them in our midst before and it is entirely possible that we will find one again. The Germans are not above reproach, and will stoop to anything, to find out how we operate and what our plans are within this compound. It is for our own protection as well as the rest of us incarcerated herein. After you find someone who can identify you, report to the officer in charge of Barracks six, room 8 and give him the name of a man who knows you personally. You have two days to accomplish this feat." With that we were dismissed and sent to the supply room to check out our equipment. I knew only too well the Germans were not above reproach when it came to smuggling in spies for they had given me some pretty good ideas, during my interrogations, as to just what extent they would go to, to achieve their goals. There seemed to be no end, to what they would be willing to do, just to get some information. I immediately approached Lt. Marlow, one of my classmates, and asked him if it would be all right to give in his name for identification purposes.

"Of course," he said, "yes I would only be too happy to have you use it." "You know," he continued, "this is really much more important than you think right now, but after you have been here for a few weeks, you will no longer question this procedure. We have caught several spies that way, and beat them up thoroughly. You can be sure the Germans lost no time in removing them from the compound. It is our only means of self protection in a place such as this. If I can help you with anything else, at any time, just let me know."

With this he departed and I started to the supply room, thinking what a small world this really was. Here, half way around the world, I had met three navigation classmates, whom I had not seen since graduation in Texas. Not the most pleasant place to meet, but still very thankful to be alive to make that reuniting possible at all, regardless of the conditions involved. Naturally I did not want to be shot down! Neither did they, but we had been, and this was no place to quibble over what you wanted. It was now up to us to make the very best of a rather trying, regrettable, unfortunate situation.

At the window of the supply room they handed me a Prisoner of War Food Parcel, two blankets, two sack covers, bowl, cup, knife, fork and spoon. With this equipment, I was to make myself happy, and manage in one way or another to keep warm during the winter that was bound to follow. As a matter of fact it was nearly upon us, it already having frozen several times. The food received was to last each until the next regular camp issue. This would take place in one week, if there were enough parcels available; if not they would issue either a ½ or ¼ parcel. If not even that many were on hand, there would be none issued, and we just tightened up our belts another notch.

The first night I spent in barracks One room 5, but the following day I saw Lt. Marlow again, and he told me that there was one bunk available in their room, block Three, room 6, so I moved in. This was a very advantageous move, for the boys had already set up their "food combine," and were working quite efficiently. It eliminated the majority of the mistakes I most assuredly would have made and got me off to a flying start under an already organized group. The room was filled with really swell fellows too, and as I was to spend the rest of my days in prison camp with them, a better set up could not have been found. I soon leaned how to budget my food too, so that it would last for the entire week, and not run out in the middle as it would most likely have done, had it not been for their careful guidance, and advice.

"There is your bunk over on the north wall, the middle one," they told me, so I walked over, placed my things on it and began taking a survey of the situation. Let's see now, soft pine boards for springs, tow sack for a mattress, and four sturdy poles to hold it up in the air above the bunk just below. Nothing choice, but better than the floor. Having made a rather complete analysis of the situation at hand, I removed my kitchen utensils, and went to work. I placed the muslin cover over the tow sack, then carefully tucked in the edges of the one thin blanket all around it. This I decided would have to do until we got further into the winter, at which time I would use the other blanket. I might just as well get used to the cold now, as prolong the evil day, and that day was bound to come in the very near future. Then too, this camp was located nearly 60 degrees north latitude, and to make matters even worse, on a small peninsula jutting out into the Baltic Sea. A colder more remote spot could not have been found in all of Germany.

Now that I had myself rather comfortably situated, at least as well as could be done under the conditions, I left the room to make a survey of my immediate surroundings. The first and probably the most outstanding thing about the entire camp, was the fact that we were surrounded by water on three sides. It did not come up to the perimeter fence, but was plainly visible about a half mile distant. Sail boats and fishing schooners were out in it this very minute. But coming closer home, or better said over the perimeter fence, about forty feet high, were the guard towers. The towers were from about a hundred to a hundred and fifty yards apart, and were completely enclosed in glass. In short the man in them could see equally well in any direction he desired. There were no blind spots. None! The towers were equipped with three flood lights, two of these were powered by electricity, and were used at all times, except in emergencies when there was no electricity available. Then the battery light was used. It rarely happened that the electric ones went out of order, for they had them wired to three different series of wires. If we succeeded in cutting one, they would still have two series to operate on. If we should succeed in cutting two they would still be going "full blast" on the one complete circuit. And if we should by any chance succeed in cutting that, they still had the battery operated light. So the chance of ever getting out all the lights was so negligible that it was rarely given a second thought.

The guard also had at his disposal a telephone with which he could contact headquarters, or any of the other towers if at any time he deemed it advisable. In the way of arms, other than his own rifle, he had a mounted machine gun, and hand grenades. The latter were there to be used only when they expected a mass break, or some other attempt on the towers themselves. How they figured that out I do not know, and did not worry about it either, for it is a sure thing we would never tell them when and if we got ready.

Beside the lights on the towers there were lights about every 75 feet along the perimeter wire on high poles, wired by the same system. As close to a fool proof system as could be found, and never did they go without lights entirely.

The perimeter fences, of which there were two, were between twelve and fourteen feet high and passed right beneath the towers. The tall fences, were covered with barbed wire running both vertically and horizontally, leaving an opening (somewhere in the vicinity of) four inches square. Between them was a space of about six feet. This had been dug to a depth of ten or twelve inches, and salted down, so no weeds would grow. In here they placed a barbed wire entanglement approximately six feet high. They did not aim for us to get out. That much was readily discernable, and as though that in itself were not enough, they placed a single strand of wire, known as a warning wire, two feet high and twenty five feet inside the main perimeter fence. If you so much as touched this or stepped over it, without first securing permission from the guard in the tower, you were shot without question. To ever get to the outside fences and start cutting your way out was a virtual impossibility. Between each of the towers, walked a sentry with his rifle. For an able assistant he was given a "man eating dog." These dogs ranged in height from three to four feet, and were extremely vicious. They are trained daily on a dummy dressed as either an American or British soldier, and they literally ripped it to shreds. I saw one of them snap a leg completely off the dummy during his session with it. That was enough for me, I decided I would rather walk on mine. I would much prefer to deal with a guard when time came for an attempted escape, for I could talk to them should I get caught in the act. I fear the dog would not listen to reason.

The camp itself, was divided into four compounds, South, North I, North II, of which I was a member, and North III. Each had approximately 2500 men and its own Allied Commanding Officer, plus a German Commanding Officer. Over the compound allied officer was the camp allied officer, and over him was the German Camp Kommondant. Through this chain the orders were disseminated to the various groups. You were not permitted to pass from one compound to the other without written permission from the German commanding officer of our compound, and this was almost impossible to get, unless you had a very good reason. Usually if you had that reason you did not care to give it to him for it was none of his business any way, so you just stayed "put."

Our compound contained nine one-story barracks of wood construction, two latrines and washrooms combined, a small laundry room and a "sump" (cesspool to you). It covered an area of a little more than a block, and in it more than 2000 men were going to have to eat, sleep and keep themselves from going "berserk," in one fashion or another. How it was going to be done, I did not know, but surely there would be some solution forthcoming in the days ahead. I had seen about all that I cared to see on my first rather thorough tour of the place, so I returned to my room to see what might be going on. Most of the others had gathered there, too by this time for the dinner hour had drawn nigh, and no one cared to miss it. We had two benches in the room capable of accommodating four each. That left the rest of us to shift for ourselves, and so we usually hit the "sack." It was either that or the floor, for it was extremely cold. Our barracks were all built on stilts and stood an average of four feet from the ground. This gave the cold wind ample opportunity to cool off the entire building, and make the floor decidedly unpleasant for sitting purposes. The table, which stood in the center of the room, would accommodate ten at one sitting if we could find something for the two men to sit on, who were unfortunate enough to get the ends. To remedy this situation we took the doors off a cupboard we had, and put each door across the ends of said bench. This settled it once and for all, and hereafter we would have definite places to sit when meal time rolled around.

In the corner stood the small triangular stove, on which all our cooking was done, and over it this very minute the cook for the "south combine" was slaving, preparing dinner, for himself, and the other nine men who belonged to his group. As soon as he had finished and set his food upon the table to be divided equally among the ten bowls lined up there, the cook for the "north compound," of which I was a member began preparing his meal. By the time the "south" had finished eating their dinner, ours was ready to be moved to the table and parceled out. The division was an all important task, and had to be done with the greatest fairness, for at best we all got very limited rations, and were losing weight daily.

In order to clarify for you what the combine system was and why it originated, I shall deviate from the story and go into it in a little more detail. It was established for many reasons, the chief one being that there was only room for ten at the table at one time. It seemed hardly fair to ask the others to go to their beds and eat. Then too, we had such a small stove that it was next to impossible to cook for more than ten men at a time, and still keep the food reasonably warm. Ten men belonged to each combine, and one of those ten, who liked to cook, volunteered to take over the job. It then became his sole responsibility to ration out all food that came in so it would last until more arrived, regardless of how long it might be between "spells." The division was accomplished very easily, for every time something came it was split fifty-fifty with the combine, for they had just as many members as we did. The cook's duties were cooking and rationing food. Nothing else was required of him for he was already doing plenty. The rest of us took care of the K.P., vegetable peeling, water carrying, floor sweeping, stove firing, etc. We had a very good system, in that each day, one man per combine was assigned to take over all the other chores, and be the cook's aid. That day he would be busy all day, but then he would have off until the remaining eight had served, after which he was due for the labor shift again. The one combine was named the "north," and the other the "south," to have an all inclusive name to shout out when meal time finally arrived. It never had to be called out twice, and no one ever forgot to which combine he belonged. On one day the north would eat first, on the next the south, thus there was never any argument or favoritism shown, as to who had the best time to eat. Here above any place else everything had to be fair, no partiality dare be shown any man, or group of men. If it did, it would only end up in an argument or a fight, and things were bad enough as they were not alone provoking additional hard feelings.

"North up," Red Turner shouted, and everyone stopped what he was doing and came dashing to the table. In less than five minutes the bowls were empty and the table was bare. "Well, that is it for tonight, pleasant dreams." Yea, I thought, on virtually an empty stomach. But for that no one in here was to blame, least of all the cook, for there was no more to be had. I sat around, talked awhile and then retired, promising myself that tomorrow I would attempt to make a pan, the likes of which we were in very dire need of. Roll call and breakfast over, found me doing just that. The Germans had not supplied us with any cooking utensils whatsoever, thus it became necessary for us to shift for ourselves, that is if we wanted to cook any of our food and we wanted to do just that. Apparently the Germans did not care if we ever got it in an edible condition. My first task then was to get some tin cans, and these I secured from the incinerators. After cleaning the cans up, I opened them with the aid of a table knife, cut the edges straight with the same instrument, and then seamed the strips together. This process I continued until I had a large enough sheet for the desired pan, at which time I laid out the proposed pattern, marked it lightly with a "scribe," made by sticking a needle in a wooden handle, then folded it along the lines indicated. Actually it was not quite that simple, and definitely not that fast, that is if you wanted to make a decent one. To make a pan would require a full day's labor, with several cut fingers thrown in for good measure. The latter was remedied in due time, by practice, and by using a bit more caution than had been the case in the earlier stages of the game. At first it seemed almost impossible to make pans from tin cans without any tools whatsoever, except a table knife. Especially without tin snips and pliers, but with ardent practice and painstaking persistence the job was accomplished. And the truth of the matter is that some really nice ones were turned out too. So nice that it would be rather hard to believe that there were no tools other than the common table knife used to do the job. Thus it went with anything we wanted. First, it became necessary to sit down and figure out a way that the proposed project could be built with the materials and tools available. Then its construction began, all of which helped to take up time, keep the mind and body reasonably alert, and make the days go faster.

Cake pans, buckets and pie tins too were made in the same manner. If you are by any chance wondering where the tin was secured, and I have little doubt that you are, I might tell you it came from the cans contained in the Red Cross food parcels. I doubt if they had any idea just how important those cans would become to prisoners when they packed the parcels, for it does not seem likely that they would have to take into consideration such a need, but we could never have existed without the cans or the food packed therein.

I was by no means the only one in the room who undertook the task of making pans. Not by any stretch of the imagination. Nearly everyone tried making one, at some time or another during our stay there, but by far the greatest contributors to the cause were "Scratch" Overdorff, "Red" Turner, "Gop" Goplin and "Hank," the 'Hunke' Kardis. Everyone's efforts were greatly appreciated and much praise went to the men for their splendid efforts in that direction. My eyes were tired as a result of looking at the bright tin all day, and I had no desire to strain them any further, so retired for the night. At the sound of the bugle, 0630 A.M. I struggled from bed, put on my clothes and prepared for the seige (roll call). After awakening the more sound sleepers in the room, some of whom it seemed could never hear the bugle, I hurriedly departed. I had no more than reached the door, when the 0650 or fall out bugle blew. Every plan I might have had, was foiled now, so I swung the barrack doors open, and walked over to the parade ground, there to be greeted by the block C.O., Capt. Jaynes.

"Good morning, Capt."

"Arrived a bit early this morning did you not?"

"Well, I could not sleep and for lack of something better to do, got up and walked around the compound. I find the fresh air much more invigorating than that bunk. You know, that thing they call a bed."

"I know that only too well."

"But it's better than the floor."

"That's debatable, at least the floor is solid."

He had me there, so I stepped back into the formation which he called to attention. Followed immediately by "Close interval, Dress right dress," We lined up in five ranks and dressed down. Upon completion of the process he gave us "At Ease," which position we assumed. The German C.O. and his counters had entered the compound and were making their way to the spot where we had gathered. The bugle blared once more signaling his immediate appearance, upon which Col. Spicer, Compound C.O., called us all to attention. The ranking German officer stepped forward, exchanged salutes with the Col. and the counting was under way. When they had completed the rounds, they gathered into a huddle. Something must be wrong. They re-checked the figures. Still the proper number was not forthcoming. There was but one alternative. The counting must be done over. Either they get the right figure or recount till they do. There is no in-between mark. After an hour they must have arrived at the designated number, for the German C.O. stepped forward, exchanged salutes once more and we were dismissed. Free once more to go back to our barracks.

What delicacy will breakfast provide me with this morning, I wondered, but not for long, for as I entered the room there it was on the table, two slices of bread. Not the kind you are accustomed to seeing either, for these were very thin, so thin in fact that they held a close resemblance to tissue paper. To read a paper through them would not have proven the least difficult. Each loaf we received, and they were standard size, was cut in from sixty to eight pieces, depending entirely upon the texture of the bread. You can see from that, there was not much there, but the fact remains that there was much more satisfaction in eating two thin slices, than one thicker one. At least the number was greater and we had to reach twice instead of once. I finished off in two minutes flat and left the table for fear I might start in on the boards!

The sun was shinning brightly so I decided today would be a good one to do my washing. At least it would dry. I gathered up my soiled clothing, took a bar of soap from my Prisoner of War Capture Kit, and made my way to the small laundry room. If only I had gotten the idea an hour earlier I might have saved myself several hours, for what should greet my eyes as I entered the room but a waiting line of twelve deep. This was nothing unusual though, and the only way to avoid such a thing would be to get up and start doing your laundry before roll call, thus get a tub before the rush hour. Once roll call was over it was too late to think about such a thing, for all the early birds had gotten them. Next time I would know better and be one of those birds. I waited patiently, and when my turn finally came threw my clothes into the concrete tub, turned on the faucet, and the freezing water came streaming forth. I still wonder how it ever got out of the faucet in a liquid form, but somehow it managed to flow. All set to go to work. What a dreadful thought. Already I was shivering, just thinking about putting my hands in that cold, cold water. But thinking about it did little good, so I started in. First I soaped it thoroughly, and by the time I had that finished, I managed to borrow a wash board, on which to scrub it. There were only six scrub boards and twelve tubs, so you can well imagine just what a problem some two thousand or more "Kriegies" had getting their washing done. I scrubbed and rubbed, my fingers and hands got colder and colder. Soon I could not bend them at all. There was but one alternative. I took my hands out, dried them off, and stuck them in my pockets. Washing under such conditions was indeed trying, and to some so discouraging that they left it go altogether. But the majority of the men washed in the near freezing water in spite of the hardships it involved. My hands had regained some of their former warmth, and my clothes had soaked during the waiting process, so I had not lost too much time. If only

I had some of that magic soap they advertise in the States, this rubbing would not be necessary, I thought to myself, but it did not help the matters at hand one bit. The only way to get this job done was to dig right in and do it, so I again braved the water. I finished the scrubbing process after considerable energy had been expended and drained the tub. Now, only the rinsing and wringing remained and this meant more of that cold fresh water. My teeth chattered in "Cadence" at the very thought of it, but at this point there remained but one thing to do, grit them and go through with it for the job was nearly finished. I rinsed the clothes, drained the tub once more and called one of the boys to come over and give me a hand wringing them. He called back that he was busy at the moment so I wrapped them around the spigot, and wrung it dry myself. Ah, yes here is the last sock, just the piece I've been looking for, and with it wrung out, I gathered my clothes together, summoned the man next in line, and left the room. Washday was over for another week. As I walked to the barracks I was thinking how nice it would be to hang it on the warning wire to dry, but only thinking mind you, for to actually do it might prove disastrous. More than likely it would eliminate all future washdays, and much as I hated the job I was in no hurry to get rid of it in such a manner. Nope, I'd hang it on a shoestring stretched out along the barracks, for that very purpose. Then after one side had dried I would go out and turn it around and give the other side an equal opportunity to do so. By nightfall, if the sun pulled no shenanigans, it would be dry. Well at least I hoped it would be, and more than that I was powerless to do. One man with a washing machine at this camp could have made a fortune, had he accepted IOU's in lieu of payment.

"North Up," I heard through the wall, so I lost no time getting into the room and to the table, where all the other "wolves" had gathered and were eagerly awaiting their portion of the food to be served. Food was very scarce, and the meal was of the same order. We did a bit better than we had at breakfast having had 2 ½ slices of bread and a cup of coffee. "So satisfying." "So filling." Yes, a good appetizer. As I was finishing my coffee, I glanced out of the window and saw a German guard walking across the compound. This gave me an idea. Maybe I could get some news from that fellow, if I approached him right. My German was not as good as it might have been, but I could manage to make myself understood. Then too, the more I practiced the better I became. Perhaps by the time I got ready to leave I might be able to speak it like a veteran. I stuck some cigarettes in my pocket to use as bait and made my exit. I glanced hastily around the compound and spotted him walking along the beaten path, parallel to the warning wire. Not wishing to make my mission too obvious I started for the path and walked leisurely down it until I had overtaken him, then walked aimlessly at his side.

"Good afternoon."

"Good afternoon," he replied.

"Do you always have such fine weather here?" I inquired.

"Oh no, this is exceptional; it gets very bad here in the winter."

I suspected as much, for being practically surrounded by the Baltic it could be no other way. When cold and warm air clash there is bound to be a storm, and this looked to me like a perfect setup for such a condition.

"And when does all this take place?"

"It will begin most any time now, and last all winter."

Now that I had him in a talkative mood, I switched subjects, knowing full well I would never secure any information relative to battle fronts talking about the weather.

"How is the war coming along?"

He closed up like a clam. No sir, I would get no information from him regarding that. But I did not give up, for after all, guards were good for something else beside war news. So I started in on another subject which had been disturbing me more than a little of late.

"By the way," I inquired, "do you know anything about any German organizations in the United States?" Now to you that may sound like a strange question to put to a German guard, but during one of my interrogations one of the questioners intimated that they had well organized groups working in the United States, and that they were pretty much out in the open while doing it. So I aimed to find out from the common man if at all possible.

"Yes, I know a little," he replied.

So I proceeded to question him further on the subject and when we had finished the conversation I had secured from him this information. He said that in essence the German American Bund was nothing more or less than the Nazi Party in disguise and not only did they have such a group in the United States, but they had them in other nations as well. He frankly told me that in his opinion this is where the Nazi party made their one big mistake, for he doubted very seriously whether we would have entered the war as early as we did had it not been for the discovery of these organizations and their aims and objectives. He further intimated that had we waited three months longer before entering the war, things would have taken on a much different atmosphere here in the United States for big things were to happen to our industries. Just what they were I do not know, nor would he reveal, but my guess is sabotage on such a large scale as to have made previous efforts in that direction look infinitesimal in comparison.

From here we turned to still another subject. I was in dire need of a good razor, some blades, and a hone if I could get them for a reasonable price.

"Could you get me a good razor, a few blades, and a hone?"

"That depends," he said, "on how much you are willing to pay."

"But I have no money, you know that."

"Ah yes, I know only too well, but you do have cigarettes, and I have none."

I just knew he was coming to that, but thought I had better let him suggest it himself, for this way he did the asking.

"Well how many cigarettes do you want?"

"I think I can spare a few."

I could spare any number for I didn't smoke at all, but why tell him that?

"I will do it for 20 cigarettes."

"That's good enough for me. You bring it in the next time you visit the compound and I will meet you as I did today."

I gave him a cigarette just to show my good faith, and with that departed. I had failed to get the battlefront news, but had managed to get some vital information and make a very good trade, so my efforts were not in vain. Whether he would deliver the goods or not, was another question, but either he did or went without the cigarettes. If he did not bring them I would have done with him, just as we did with other snoopers who did not cooperate, slip a few cigarettes into his pocket, unknown to him, and when he left, follow him up to the gate. Once he got in the forelager I would simply call the commanding German Officer's attention to the cigarettes he had in his pocket, and he would be promptly searched. When those cigarettes made their appearance, and they were bound to for he would not even know he had them, off to solitary he would go for a week's siege. Not the best way, but very effective. After all if he came in primarily and solely for the purpose of snooping he meant to do us no good, so we in return aimed to make both his life and job extremely distasteful. If on the other hand I found that he did deliver the articles asked for I would treat him with respect and continue getting things from him, making it profitable for him and comfortable for myself and the others whom I might be able to help out. Each guard was carefully checked and tried many times before he was ever fully trusted, and the extent of the trust placed in him depended entirely upon how far he was willing to go to get things in that were highly prized by us, and definitely against the regulations by the Germans. He could take his choice. I had driven my bargain, and had nothing to lose.

Two days later he returned—I met him, and together we went to the laundry room to transact our business. If he were caught bringing anything into the compound, he would be sent to solitary confinement for two weeks. Not particularly desirous of spending time in the clink he secreted the articles well in his clothing, thus eliminating the chance of discovery while passing through the gates into the compound. Guards were periodically searched before entering the compound itself, to prevent just such a thing, but they liked cigarettes so well that most of them were willing to take the chance, and accept the consequences, should they be caught in the act. He reached into a hidden pocket and withdrew his hand. There were the very things I had asked for. A nice shiny new nickel-plated razor, five blades and a hone. Just like the doctor ordered, so I handed him his pack of cigarettes and thanked him for his trouble. He asked me if there was anything further I wanted, but as I had no needs for the present, other than food, and that he would not bring anyway, I told him no.

"I shall remember you though, and if at any future time I find myself in need of something, I will look you up. Good day," I said, and went back to my room to show the boys the results of my trade. Upon examination they were all of the opinion that I had gotten a real bargain, especially in the hone, for there was not another in the barracks. It was indeed a luxury and a highly prized piece of equipment. Just then the bugle blew, indicating that evening roll call was just some fifteen minutes away. After much shuffling in the crowded room I managed to get my coat and knit cap and walked out to the "Parade Ground," there to go through the same process as I had in the morning. Roll call twice a day soon became very monotonous, but it made little difference for it went on in spite of what I thought. Then too, there were those days when they had three roll calls, just broke the routine. Well at least we got some fresh air.

"Dismissed," the Col. shouted, and I was off like a light, only to find myself back in the crowded room with twenty equally hungry men. Yes sir, it was dinner time, and this was the meal of meals, the "main stay of the day." At least there would be something beside bread. "The Vultures" were standing around the table "calipering" up the bowls by eye, as the cook was measuring them out as to the very best of his ability. In a matter of minutes another would meet it's Waterloo. If there ever were a group of men who could tell at a glance which bowl had two drops more than the other, I do believe they lived in this prison camp. Make no mistake about it, everyone was interested in seeing that justice was done for all, but was doing a royal good job of looking out for himself at the same time. This, it seemed, was the only way to survive the ravages of war in a prison camp surrounded by barbed wire, where your only source of nourishment was that food brought in to you. Upon completion of the division, came the familiar sound "North up" and everyone crawled over the bench, sat down, and began eating lustily. A half bowl of potato soup mixed with vegetables that had been cooked at the same time, two thin slices of bread, and a cup of tea. Ah, but it was good, at least it filled a spot for the time.

Tomorrow, was my day for "K.P." so without further hesitation, I went to bed. I wanted a good night's sleep before taking on those chores, so I might be ready, willing and able.

At the crack of dawn I was up and after dressing, went over to the corner, removed the ashes from our small stove, using the shovel I had made for that express purpose. By this time my able assistant from the "South combine" had gotten up too, and together we swept the floor, with our makeshift brooms. The brooms were made of twigs fastened securely together with bits of wire or tin. I never saw either a broom or mop as long as I was in camp, and that was approximately nine months. Surely they must have had some, but were not predisposed to give us any. It might have made our work a bit easier, and the task of keeping the room clean, less burdensome. I don't believe they saw eye to eye with us, when it came to making life more comfortable, anyway they did very little in that direction.

After breakfast they put me on the "Water wagon" which meant carrying water from the washroom to the barracks, but as it was my day to be the cook's aide I said nothing. Just did as I was requested. I had no more than finished that errand and sat down, when "Red" handed me two boxes of "C" Ration Biscuits to crush. They were "square cracker shaped affairs" and very hard. To eat them in this condition gave one very little satisfaction, so they were crushed into flour and baked into a cake. This was done by laying them flat on the table, and then skidding back and forth over the top with a cup, much the same as you would with a rolling pin, grinding the biscuits into powder. As I was working I commenced to think that surely there must be some easier and quicker way to do this job than the one I was now using. The more thought I gave it the more certain I was that it would be done in a more satisfactory method and as the day progressed, the idea of a machine for the purpose began to take shape. With that I passed over it for the time being, for I would have more than enough to do today without attempting an additional job. But at my first opportunity I promised myself that I was going to begin work on the machine and see whether it could be done or not. I succeeded in getting the biscuits well crushed in about an hour and a half, after which they were scraped up and put into a bowl. There water was mixed with the crumbs plus powdered milk, fifteen ounces of prunes, and a dash of tooth powder. The latter was used in lieu of baking powder. It did not work too successfully, but helped; anyway it stimulated our imagination. The batter was then thoroughly mixed, put into a pan made expressly for cake baking, and inserted into the oven to bake. The oven too was the product of tin cans. Literally hundreds of them that had been collected from the incinerators went into that oven, and even more hours of work. Its construction consisted of making two metal boxes, one enough smaller than the other so that it would slip inside and still leave approximately an inch and a half on all sides for circulating, with the exception of the front, where a sliding metal door was placed. The oven was then placed about eighteen inches above the stove and connected to the pipe rising from it. On the top of the oven we secured the elbow which diverted the smoke into the chimney. Through this enclosed space the smoke from our small stove traveled and in so doing provided the inner box with sufficient heat to do the baking.

After lunch, Lt. Jones and I washed the cups, knives and whatever else had been used, and then proceeded to peel and dice the potatoes, which were to be cooked for the evening meal. It was necessary for the potatoes to be on the stove by two, if we wished to get them in an edible condition by five, for it was a very slow heater and took every bit of three hours to accomplish the job. Once I had them on the stove they became the cook's responsibility, so I worried no more about them. I did fire up occasionally, but other than that left them strictly alone.

The remainder of the afternoon passed rapidly and it was not long before that beloved task of washing the bowls, cups, knives, forks, spoons and pans used for the evening meal stared me in the face. I did not particularly mind though, for usually the more there were dirtied the more we had had to eat, and that was the really important issue. "Food," that which we never got enough of, but somehow managed to exist on. Washing the pans was the big job and the most dreaded, for there were so many seams in them. It was almost impossible to get them clean. But if we wanted to stay reasonably healthy, we could ill afford to take the chance of letting them get dirty, for that would but "heap coal" on an already undesirable situation.

With everything finally cleaned up I dashed up to the washroom, filled the bucket and pitcher with fresh water and returned to the barracks to settle down for the evening's activities. Some of the men were busy playing cards, which they had made from paper cheese boxes. Lt. Wilson, better known as "the mole" to us was cartooning on soap wrappers on bed slats, the only materials available. On one corner of the table sat Lt. Daniels and "Bo Bo" Bolinski. They were busily engaged in a game of dominoes, which the former had made from wood chips. "Scratch" Overdorff was writing like fury in his diary, so that he could again get it back to its still secret hiding place. I too was working on mine and upon completion sewed it back into the lining of my coat. There it would remain until I again decided to make an entry. Next I took out my log book, in which I was making dedications and writing poems, and began work on the memorials for the boys of my crew who I knew definitely lost their lives on that fateful day in September. I had no more than laid out the one for Lt. Baker, when the lights were turned off for the evening. Another day had come and gone! Eight o'clock had rolled around and there would be no more light until morning. They were extremely stingy with their electricity, so much so, in fact that each room had but one 25 watt bulb to light it up. Small as it was it did aid materially in keeping us from stumbling over one another in the semi dark, which might otherwise have been the case. It served still another purpose too, namely that of ruining the prisoners' eyes, if they tried to do some close work by it. Whether this was deliberately planned or not is hard to say, however I feel sure I would be safe in venturing a guess anyway, it was so planned. Thus, when Germany was defeated, and surely time would bring this about, we would be of little use to our respective countries upon return, in carrying on the war against their partner in crime, the Japanese. The Germans were really much more far sighted in those things than any of us in the United States are willing to give them credit for, much to my dismay – but even more to my sorrow and regret.

Now that the lights were out, we had one of two alternatives before us. Either we could retire, and put the body in a horizontal position, which itself was a horrible thought, for it just meant another night of freezing and discomfort, or we could light up our makeshift lamps in which we burnt margarine, when we had it to spare, and thus continue on with what we had been doing. Actually the lamp would supply nearly as much as light as the bulb anyway. But I chose to go to bed, so piled all the excess clothes I could find on top of my two thin blankets, and then crawled in. Once in the "sack" I took roll call on the slats, and this was a comparatively simple feat to accomplish. Let's see, I can feel one directly under my head, another under my shoulders, a third under my elbows, a fourth under my hips, and so it went until I got to nine. "All present and accounted for." Originally there had been ten, but one was already broken and could not be replaced. What we really needed was a "wood stretcher" but somehow or another such a machine has not yet been devised. I rolled over and tried to sleep. Yes, tried is the proper word too, for it seemed every time I was about ready to doze off into precious slumberland, I would begin to freeze either from the top or the bottom. I would roll over to warm that portion and catch about forty winks when the same process would begin to freeze either from the top or the bottom. There was just no end to it, if it was not the cold it was the bed slats. Something was always wrong but eventually morning came and the warning bugle would blow once more. Thus relief to a "weary, slat ridden" body, to say nothing of a tortured mind.

Each morning before arising I would remove the New Testament, of which I had procured a copy from the Padre, and read a chapter, thus strengthening myself spiritually for what the day might have in store. I had read it completely through twice and was well on the way the third reading, when liberation finally came. It gave me much comfort, and made living under the very worst conditions, seem not too much of a chore, but rather something to be extremely thankful for. As long as there was life there was hope, and many of the men, who no longer had that life, but lay still and quiet beneath the soil, would be only too glad to exchange places with me, had they but the opportunity. Everytime I felt abused this thought ran foremost through my mind, and there was no complaint coming forth, but only quietness and deep consideration and reverence for the members of my crew who now lay buried somewhere in Germany. At least I hoped that the German who had found the men had had that much decency and respect and at least provided them with a simple burial and a marked grave. However, I shall have to admit that at times I began to wonder whether they actually did get that last bit of respect generally shown to a corpse.

The Fall out Bugle, and me still in bed! Now was the time for action or I'd never make it. As I dashed over to the parade grounds, I wondered what this day might have in store for me, for the most of them had turned out to be nothing more or less than routine, tiresome affairs. They counted us once, they counted us twice, and still no right answer. We shivered, we froze, it was bitterly cold. The wind came tearing from the north with the anger of a ferocious lion. But all to no avail, we must remain steadfast. To the guards it made little or no difference for they had been properly fed and clothed for the occasion, but for us it was quite a different story. Had we planned it this way ourselves, and deliberately "fouled" up the roll call because we did not want them to get an accurate count it would not have been so bad, for at least we would have had the satisfaction of knowing that we were annoying them, which I shall be forced to admit was done on occasions when we deemed it unwise for them to get the proper count. We would just refuse to line up and dress down properly, thus make counting very difficult if not entirely impossible. When at that, we would be the ones who suffered the most, but for a justifiable cause. As the situation now stood things were not so rosy. We had everything to lose and nothing to gain. There must be something wrong. There was, too, for a large number of guards are entering the compound. The answer at this point is quite simple. They deliberately miscounted us so that we would be standing out there when the "search party" arrived. Thus there would be no men in the barracks hampering them while they leisurely tore apart our belongings. There was only one mystery remaining at this hour, which barracks was it going to be? That was the question. Everyone hoped it was not his. I hoped it was not ours, for I didn't relish the idea of my things thrown all over the floor. But relish it or not they were headed in that direction and sure enough it was block three. We were to be the victims of their wrath. The German Commanding Officer now dismissed us and we headed for the barracks only to be denied entrance. "Come back in about three hours" the guard told us, "and we will be through." "Go on, get away from here, you can't even stand around the barracks and watch." Standing out in the cold was not exactly appreciated either, but what else was there to do? The worst thought of all was, what were they going to do in there for three hours? Search and ransack to their heart's content, without a doubt.

Three hours later we returned. The search was over, so they brought in the cart, drove it up to the door and threw in the loot. "You see that red headed, full faced, chubby fellow over there," one of the boys said to me as they were loading the cart.

"Sure I see him. What is so interesting about him?"

"He is commonly called 'Henry the Butcher' by the prisoners of the camp."

"Well you see it's this way. Prior to the war he was a civilian butcher in the United States. There are men in this very compound who have bought meat from him, over the counter in Brooklyn, New York."

"Are you sure about that?" I said.

"I certainly am, and I can show you some of the men who have done that very thing. Have you not noticed how he glories in making life generally miserable for us?"

"Now that you speak of it, I have. I have also noticed that he speaks fluent English, but I had never quite pieced it together that way."

"You will find that to be the case alright, and if he knows what is good for him he will get a thousand miles away, once this camp is liberated, or he will be a dead pigeon. He has more enemies amongst the prisoners than any one man in this place."

"That I can believe. And from what you have told me I can see where he can add another to his already overflowing list of arch enemies."

"Those fellows, he continued, came over here with the thought in mind that Germany would surely win the war. Once that goal has been achieved they will be all set to pick off a nice big political job in the states under 'Der Fuehrer' for they are well acquainted with the habits of the people there, thus being the most likely candidates for that selection."

"Those dirty rats! Is that all a country that supplied them with their daily bread and butter meant to them? Why they should be hung as traitors to the cause."

"Hanging is too good for them," he replied. They should use a more painful method of disposing of his type. And the sad part of it is that he is by no means the only one that had pulled that trick. There are literally thousands of them, and each brought back to Germany much vital information."

"Yes, that is very true," I replied. "But maybe when this is all over we can get revenge." Quite frankly I don't think that they are going to win this war, as a matter of fact I am sure of it. There will come a day of reckoning, and when it does they had better hide. By this time they had the cart loaded and were on the way to the forelager, so we parted and both went to our respective rooms, to survey the damage.

When I got to the door I knew what had happened, for the evidence was staring me in the face. There in the center of the room was a heap of clothes, bedding, and capture parcels. What a mess. Everything was upside down. All the beds were torn up, some of the tow sacks had been slit open with a knife to see if anything had been stowed inside of them. It looked as though a cyclone had struck the place, and left nothing but litter in its wake. How anyone could be so inconsiderate, was beyond me. Clothes that had just been recently washed, were lying all over the floor. It seemed unbelievable that such a thing could happen, but here was the proof. I checked my "D" Bars and found one of them missing, also some cigarettes. Well I would remedy that. Hereafter all "D" Bars would be sewn into my clothes, that way if they wanted them they would have at least have to search me personally. As for the cigarettes I did not particularly care, for I didn't smoke anyway, so had little use for them other than to trade with. My diary they had not found, for I had it with me, but they did find the hammer one of the boys had made from a bolt. He had spent many precious hours carving a handle for it, with the idea in mind that the next time we made a pan at least there would be something with which to pound the seams together. But the Germans thought otherwise. They were afraid that they might be clubbed over the head with it rather unexpectedly sometime, so took it along as insurance that it would not happen. But oh how wrong they were, for we would make another and the next time they made a raid, there it would be staring them in the face, unless of course we succeeded in hiding it some place they could not find it, and that we aimed to do. Whether or not the hiding place proved adequate for the occasion only the next raid would tell, and another would be forthcoming in another few weeks, and that we knew for sure. Several cans of food had disappeared too, and those we could ill afford to lose for our rations were extremely thin as it was, but such are the ways of the enemy. I sincerely hope they enjoy it, for they can tell by the labels it was sent by the American Red Cross for our use. I feel certain we are in more dire need of it than they are for at least they are not surrounded with a barbed wire guard, but can go out and shift for themselves. Yes, they could even shoot a deer on Goerring's private reserve not 1 kilometer distant if they got hungry enough.

I had seen enough, so gathered up some bedding, walked over to my bed and made it. At least it would be ready to sit or lie in during the day if I chose to do so. And the way I felt right now it looked as though that might happen, but first I went across the hall to see how the boys had fared over there. They had lost a drill and file, both of which they had just recently lifted from a German workman's tool kit. That was a short-lived asset. They also lost a saw they had made, and a table knife. Down the hall still farther they lost a well-sharpened table knife that had been used for cutting the hard German bread. The Germans told them that it was too sharp and too pointed. They might stab somebody with it. Yes, they might have accidentally and you can bet it would not have been an American. And so the story went from one end of the barracks to the other. Some lost articles stowed away in the attic, for the Germans had gone up there with their flashlights, and looked in every crack, crevice and corner. They checked everything for false bottoms, sliding panels, and loose boards, but even at that missed some very carefully hidden objects. This, of course made us very happy, for even to get away with the smallest article was a great achievement. When I returned to the room the rest of the men had their bedding picked up, so at least I could complete the job, of sorting out the clothes belonging to me. A disheartening job, for it had not been more than two days ago that I had washed them. Just the thought of it ran chills up my spine. If the raid did nothing else it made plenty of work, for not alone was there laundry to do, but there were all the home made tools that had to be replaced. It seemed an endless task, for no more would the job be done, and another raid would be forthcoming. Discouraging as it was the boys never gave up, they just kept right on working. "Never say die" seemed to be their motto, and they stuck by it faithfully.

Noon, and still we had had no breakfast. "Well," said the cook, "we will just eat breakfast and dinner together. That will give you twice as much bread, and your regular cup of coffee. Perhaps then you can stand it until the evening meal." With that the K.P. took the bread to the stove, toasted it, and we ate. We had just finished when a man came to the barracks and called out "Red Cross Up." That did it. Screams of joy could be heard all over the barracks, and the men ran like wild to the rationing room, taking their bowls with them. The crowd and rush was worse than could be found on the down town streets of New York City during the Christmas shopping season. If by chance you were caught standing in the hall you would find yourself swept right on out the door in the flood of men. Food again, what a lovely thought, more tin cans too, and best of all truly delicious edibles from the States that we knew were not filled with things that might give us acute indigestion. When I arrived at the ration room, I noticed the boys working there dumping the contents of the box out on the table. The German overseer, then stepped over, picked up the salt and pepper and put in his box. This he took to the German officer's mess for their use. Occasionally the Americans working in there managed to slip one of the packets into their pockets or down their pants legs but the number they managed to get away with were very few compared to the total number. What it actually amounted to was stealing what belonged to you anyway. Once this had been done they cut open the fish can, and dumped the fish into the bowl we had brought along. The jam can met with the same fate, and I have seen them pour the jam right on top of the fish, just to be even more nauseating than they were already. All the rest of the cans were chopped into with a meat cleaver which they had there for just that purpose. When they had the cans all butchered up they were tossed back into the box and handed to us, so we might take the precious cargo back to our respective rooms. From here on out it was up to each of us individually, to figure out some formula whereby it would last until the next issue, whenever that might be. Had they not chopped into the cans, it would have been much easier, for deterioration could not have set in so quickly. However the damage was done, and the grumbling we did helped none, it was up to us to save what we would, for we could ill afford to lose anything due to spoilage. We took those cans we intended to keep for any length of time and smeared margarine over the gashes. This would for the present keep most of the air from the contents, however, at best it was only a temporary arrangement and could not be relied upon for any length of time.

The fish had to be eaten almost immediately for they had been poured from the can. We never kept them over 24 hours unless absolutely necessary. The complete contents of the parcel were put into the combine, with the exception of 4 oz. of "D" Bar, which we were permitted to keep and eat whenever the desire was the greatest. To most of the boys this was immediately and they lost no time in devouring the tasty concentrated chocolate, while others laid part of it back, for that day in the uncertain future when maybe there would be even less to eat. It did not seem that such could be the case, but when surrounded with barbed wire, guards and dogs, one can not be too sure about anything. Frankly I secreted half of mine in small pockets that I had sewn on the underside of my coat lining. The searching party had taken some once, but they would get no more if I could help it. I meant to eat it myself from here on out, if I had to wear my coat everywhere I went the remainder of my stay in prison camp. It seemed the Germans never bothered to search your person once you arrived in the camp itself, so anything carried thereon was pretty safe. If they should desire to raid the barracks some time during the day, while I was in the room I would just slip on my coat, when the man on room guard gave the alarm, signifying the entrance of the guard, and jump out the window. We were always given ample warning to make just such an exit possible, and more than once we went pouring out the windows, too. It was quite a sight and did not increase the German's love for us one bit, but they were nearly powerless to stop it unless they brought in a tremendous number of guards, and guards in such numbers they never had to spare.

After carefully packing the contents of the food parcel into the combine pantry, I left. Once out in the area I headed straight for the laundry room for I was busy gathering materials for my cracker grinder and had come to the place where I needed a wooden plug, to be used as the cylinder. There was just such a piece in the laundry room too, for I had seen it there while doing my wash several days ago. That is, it was there, whether it still would be, was yet another question. I entered and took a quick look. It was no longer where it had been. I needed that plug, for it was approximately the right size, being about 2 ½ inches in diameter and 6 inches long. This gave me some wood to whittle off, but once I found it I could manage that with a table knife I had sharpened on a brick for just such a purpose. I was nearly ready to give up, when I discovered it in a corner under a small pile of rubbish. Dirty, but nothing that a little water, plus elbow grease, would not remedy. With this accomplished I stopped at the incinerator to pick up several tin cans to be used for the casing, and then returned to the room and began work. I worked on the plug for days, taking care to get it as perfectly cylindrical as possible, and after finally completing it figured out the length of the tin that would be required to go around it. This sheet I punched full of holes with a nail, this giving it many sharp cutting edges, then seamed it together into a cylindrical form. The tin form was then slipped over the wooden plug for which it had been prepared. So tight was the fit, that further fastening was unnecessary. Next I made the two end pieces to fit on the shaft and after that the header against which the cracker would sit while being sheared away. These completed, I made the outside casing and assembled the machine. It was a beauty, if I did have to say so myself. At this time it still was of no use though, for as yet I had not made the crank and that was the all important next move. On the one end of the wooden cylinder I left both a round shoulder for the bearing and a square one on the very end for the crank, so all that remained now was for me to carve a square hole out of a strip of wood, and surely there must be a broken bed slat around somewhere for just such a purpose. Once I found it, I carved it out with my trusty table knife, and fastened it securely to the machine. I was all set to go. Either it would make me the laughing stock of the room or it would prove successful, and the next few minutes would tell the story. Almost as bad as when "Fulton" was trying out the steamboat, but try as I may to do it in privacy, the fellows in the room would have none of it.

There was but one thing to do in a case like that. Fasten it to the shelf, and try it out. This I did without further ado, and found that it worked swell. I could grind a whole box full of crackers in five minutes and formerly we had spent an hour doing the same job. What a time saver that was. Not that we had anything else to do with our time, but it gave us all a lot of satisfaction to think that something useful could be made from next to nothing. Very few raw materials, and no tools, but a lot of hard work, and much planning. This was the result, It ground the crackers much finer than had heretofore been the case with the cup and then too it was much more sanitary for it was completely covered and no dust or dirt could enter. The machine age had started in room six, block three. This job took fifteen to twenty days part time work, but brought loads of satisfaction for everyone concerned. So it was worth everything that had gone into it and then some. Many of the other boys came to the room and looked it over, then went back and made copies of it, thus lightening their work too. It served its purpose well. I was tired and for lack of something better to do, I "hit the sack." I had made myself semi-comfortable, and was about to doze off when somebody entered the room, and said that we, our room was to be on the "goon guard" tomorrow. Now that was a nice pleasant thought to retire with. Tomorrow we were to take turns at watching the entrances to the barracks, acting as alarm bells every time a German approached the building. Morning found us doing just that too, and every time a German approached, the familiar ring of a "goon up" could be heard up and down the hall. If he entered the building, and occasionally they did, the tune would change to "enemy in the barracks." That is it would change to that if you knew what was good for you, for if they heard you calling them goons, you would have a one way ticket to the "cooler." There you could sit down, relax, and think it over for a spell. "There" as one of the Germans himself so aptly put it, "you could ponder over the situation in peace and quiet, and decide whether they were goons or not." Regardless of how much thinking was done on the situation, you still came up with the same inevitable conclusion, namely that they were goons, but maybe you had better not voice your opinion too loudly while in their presence or you would just make a return trip, for a more extended visit. At one time during our stay at camp, the waiting list was so long for solitary, that you had to wait three months before you could serve your sentence. Nobody liked solitary confinement that well, but everyone hated the Germans so intensely that they felt a good insult in their direction was worth the price. Once in the "cubicle" the only one you could bother was the guard, and after a time he would have nothing to do with you either, so that left but the four bleak barren walls to stare at, the favorite past time of all "Kreigies," for regardless whether you were in solitary or not, that was about all there was to be done. The only notable difference was that in the compound itself you had someone to talk to, while in solitary supposedly no one was about. The walls may have had ears, but they certainly did not talk back.

The day soon passed by and night was again upon us. What to do with our nights was quite a problem, but this evening, that did not particularly disturb us for we had received our allotment of "writing forms." Everyone was sitting around trying to think of something to write home. There were only two pencils in the room so we had to take turns in doing the actual writing, but getting something in mind to write was still another thing. You could not very well tell what the real conditions were, for in the first place the Germans would not let them go through if you did, and in the second place had they done so, I doubt very seriously whether many of the boys would have written what was transpiring anyway, for it would just cause unnecessary worry once the letters were delivered. Whether the letters would ever be delivered or not, we did not know, all we could do was to write and hope. The rest was up to someone else. What a problem. There were so many things you wanted to say, but could not due to censorship; still other things you might like to mention would jeopardize your future plans in camp. Then too, the space for writing was very limited, so our choice of material must be specific and to the point.

As I glanced about the room this is the sight that greeted my eyes. Men were everywhere. Five of them were sitting at the table pondering over their forms, one was sitting by the stove on a stump of wood we had stolen; mute, apparently worlds away in thought. Probably at home right this minute. Others were in their "sacks" with feet folded beneath them like pigeons on their favorite roost. Still others gave the appearance that they literally were hanging from the ceiling by their hair, but actually were sitting on their third story bunks, which were just some 24 inches from the ceiling. Everyone of them without a doubt had taken his mind back to the United States and his loved ones for the present, and so in body only was at this minute in prison camp. Did our parents, wives, sweethearts and friends know we were here, or didn't they? Or on the other hand did they believe us to be dead? That was a question we could not answer, for we had no way of knowing, and so was just another of those indefinite things about prison camp. Things that you could only pray would happen, but would never have the satisfaction of knowing for sure whether they did or not. But as time went on some of us found the answers, while others still were wondering when the final curtain came down, and release was at the doorstep.

In the final analysis the position assumed by the various members had little affect on the letters for in one manner or another they were all written even though the obstacles seemed insurmountable at the beginning. Once the task had been completed everyone was as happy as could be under the circumstances, which needless to say was not too good, for those cherished memories of home brought to mind many things we were not so sure we would ever be privileged to see again.

Lights out hour had arrived and so off to the bunks we went, which to me was no job at all for I had been sitting in mine writing the letters, while to some of the others it necessitated a few steps to get from wherever they might have been perched to their bunks proper. In a few more minutes all was quiet, until someone mentioned the subject of faithfulness on the part of wives and sweethearts in the States. That was about all it took to get a good argument, and so a heated discussion ensued each in turn expressing his opinion in the case. As for coming to a conclusion on the subject, that was still another thing. It would all boil down to individual cases, for we well knew that different people would react differently under various situations. There it was dropped and we tried to gather in a bit of "shut eye" only to be awakened by the siren blowing outside. An air raid was in the making, all of which made us very happy, as long as they missed us, for the more the enemy was bombed the greater the destruction to their war plants, and the weaker they became, with the result that our day of release was that much closer at hand. Anyway these were the conclusions that we had drawn and for that you could not rightly blame us, for liberation was the day we were living for. It was the one thought foremost in our minds. We never worried particularly about being bombed by our own forces, once we arrived in camp, for we were well aware that they knew where we were. As a matter of fact I had seen aerial photos of this camp about a month before being shot down, but never did I dream I would take up residence there. Just proves to you that you can not be too sure what will happen next.

The sirens continued to wail, and soon the perimeter lights on the entire camp were turned out, all of which brought a sudden stillness and death like silence to the entire area. We could hear the hum of the engines as the bombers approached, and as they neared the hum grew louder and louder. Our hearts beat with an excessively firm throb, at times nearly skipping a beat. Every man, as he was lying in his bed, was offering a silent prayer, in behalf of the men who were up there—asking that they be led safely to their target and back home again, so it might be possible to return on another night for just the same purpose. Selfish prayers, yes, but some of the most earnest ones I have ever heard. Those of us in this camp, had not been that fortunate but we surely wanted the men who still remained to carry out the job we were now unable to do. Not so long ago we too had been part of that great team, and we longed for the day when we could get out and again set foot in a free world. For those who remained free we asked the best of luck and God's guidance and protection so they might keep hitting the enemy day and night. Forever onward they must go until the enemy got tired of it and called for mercy.

Now that they had passed safely overhead, the anxiety dropped to a lower level, and the conversation took on a renewed emphasis. We all wondered just where they were going and what type bombs they might be carrying, but in our present predicament we would have to do without those answers. We could only guess, and that brought little satisfaction. Just the thought of it, though did recall to our minds a rather amusing incident which happened while we were still flying. It seems the Germans took pride in the thought that they were "quite sharp" when it came to camouflage work, and so efficient had they become, at least so they thought, that they built an entire "dummy city," factories and all, just about five miles from the real one. They labored and toiled for months going into great detail so we would not discover the ruse while we watched closely just what they were doing. After they finally had it completed smokestacks and all, we sent a heavy bomber force over, just as they had hoped we would. But the story is not yet ended! In several of the bombers they carried wooden bombs, while in the rest they had the real "McCoy." Once they arrived at the target those carrying the wooden bombs flew over the "fake city" and dropped them on it, while the rest of the planes dropped their deadly load on the real plants. To the Germans it undoubtedly was no joke, but to us it was very amusing and we had a good laugh at their expense, for they had spent many hours, days, weeks and months in the hope that they might fools us, and then when the test came they found that their efforts had met with complete and utter failure. And not alone had we discovered the lark, but to add irony to insult had dropped wooden bombs on it. Had we left it undisturbed it would not have been so bad but to drop wooden bombs on it was about the greatest insult that we might have conveyed upon them. I have little doubt but that it was the most heart breaking incident in the annals of German camouflage. What a fatal blow to German prestige!

In about an hour the planes that had passed over were returning from the target and were homeward bound once more. Again we prayed that they might all be spared from "Ack Ack" in their path, and guided safely back to their respective bases. Where those bases might be we had no way of knowing, but rather suspected they must be somewhere in England, unless they had been changed quite recently. That did not seem likely to me for to move a giant bomber base takes much time and even more equipment. After they had been gone some fifteen minutes the outside lights again came on, and feeling there was no further need to stay awake, we rolled over and went to sleep. But the Germans had other ideas about the situation and decided there must be some checking up done now, for no telling just how many men might have gotten away during the air raid when all was dark. Apparently they did not trust their guards nor dogs any too well when visibility was limited due to the lack of lights. Why, I shall never know for they usually doubled them every time it happened. Besides, to get over the fence or through it past all the guards without detection was well nigh impossible.

They turned on the lights in the barracks and started their "Kriegie No. check." What a system they had. They would station two guards in the hall to see that no one ran from one room to the other during the check. Two other men would do the actual checking, one counting heads as the ranking men secured the POW numbers. It was exasperating to even think of getting up at this hour of the morning on a floor covered with frost and a room cold as ice, but you never really thought much about the situation, but rather did as you were commanded, for "rifle triumphs over spoon." They had all the odds on their side. We rolled out and when the guard entered the room with his able assistant, snapped to attention. He gave us ease, took his pad and pencil and proceeded down the list. He called out our names and we in turn answered with our prisoner numbers. This gave him the necessary assurance we were the right men, and secondly that none had escaped. You might wonder what prevented us from learning the next man's number and giving it, just in case he did escape. The answer to that is quite simple. Twenty men answered, there must be twenty heads for the counter. If not, well the solution would be obvious. Well you might say, what prevented you from using the outside window and going from one room to another that way. Nothing much except that dog and the guard that were standing outside. I am not so sure the guard would shoot you immediately, but to face that vicious dog, would have been sheer suicide. I did not want to sacrifice my arm or leg for such an animal's appetite; frankly I preferred to retain them in their present status. But aside from that there were still other methods to get the job done, and they were used. Just what they were will never be mentioned, but will be left for the next man to figure out for himself once he gets in a spot such as that. If you never get in such a predicament you won't need the knowledge, once you do, you can figure your own way out. The reason for taking this stand is quite simple and to illustrate let me cite to you just what I mean.

After World War I and it had not been too long ago, the Germans sent men over here to visit and talk with many of the men who escaped their prison camps during that war. They assembled all the information they could and when they had their files as complete as they could get them, they returned to Germany and put the information in safekeeping. Along comes World War II. They will again have to build prison camps. So they go to their previously gathered data, information that men gave them never once stopping to think what they had done, and build the camps fool proofing every method to escape used in the first great World War. That as you can readily see made escape a very difficult problem this time. Yes, it is quite true that a few men made heroes of themselves telling all they knew and showing JOHN Q. PUBLIC just how clever they really were, but at the same time they did prisoners of this war just past, one of the greatest injustices that could ever have been done. All for the sake of a little glory, which at best is comparatively short-lived, and to build up their ego in the community in which they lived. What they did for the Germans was apparently never given any consideration or thought. Had it been, this disaster could have been averted and a larger portion of our men could have escaped incarceration thus returning to our own lines to help the noble cause. We do not intend to make that blunder again.

The Kregie number check completed, they turned out the lights, and so we were permitted to sleep uninterrupted until morning, which was not many hours away any more. But it really made little or no difference for once roll call was over we could again return to our "sacks" if we so desired, as there was nothing that demanded our attention, except those unlucky fellows on K.P., and of course that excluded me for I had just had that job several days ago, so would not have it again for a week.

With the dawn of the new day the sun was shining brightly, so at least there was one thing cheerful about the compound. Further, a clear sky definitely meant that the war would be carried on with a clear sky with all its fury from the air, that is if the same conditions prevailed over the fronts, that was evident here and that condition we profoundly hoped, existed. Roll call went off without a hitch and so back to the barracks and back to the sack to catch up on all that rest I missed out on last night, but to even try to sleep in the daytime with so many fellow in the room is a chore in itself, unless you are deaf in one ear and can't hear out of the other, and as yet I had not reached that condition. Nevertheless I did lie down, for the relaxation in itself would help some. About noon I arose and partook of the usual two sandwiches, and then started for the front gate where the men were already lining up to go to the show "Getting Sentimental Over You," which was to be given in the North I Compound Hall. After standing and waiting for an hour or so the Germans finally managed to get us counted whereupon they opened the gates and marched us into the forelager, where we were again halted and counted. After arriving at a number, the "devil" only knows that, they opened the main gates and marched us down to North I Compound forelager where the same thing went on again, so after much fuss, feathers and ado we were permitted into the hall where the show was ready to begin. Talk about your red tape in the American Army, well the Germans have more than their share of it, too.

The show was a musical and was put on by the men of North I Compound, who had been here some time already, and had managed to assemble enough instruments to have an orchestra, and also enough men who desired to sing to have a chorus. It was indeed excellent and certainly brought tears to many of our eyes for it brought back stronger than ever before the memories of the States, and all that we now had lost contact with and would be unable to reestablish friendship with for some time to come in the future. The music was all written and arranged by men who had been taken prisoners, and the entire orchestra and chorus were made up of men who had met a like fate. In short it was an all prisoner show, as would be any that might follow it. The instruments that the orchestra used were sent in by the international YMCA and were certainly a blessing in disguise. They would supply us with the only version of good old United States music, for the remainder of our stay in camp, with the exception of course of the recordings also sent in by the same organization. These were played periodically in the group office for those who desired to hear the proposed program. Many thousands attended regularly.

The show over, we again lined up in formation and after the usual counting and recounting and opening and shutting of a number of gates, four to be exact, we finally arrived back in our own compound and were turned loose, so that we might return to our own barracks. Night was upon us and we retired.

Saturday arrived and with it a little unexpected excitement. At three in the afternoon, with apparently everything up to "par," we noticed a plane come dashing over the landscape heading straight for Barth which was 3 Km south west of us. Not an air raid siren had sounded, no antiaircraft guns were shooting. What could be wrong? Either radar had not picked it up or the men operating the apparatus were asleep for it was a British mosquito that came streaking over Barth at tree top height strafing as it went down the main street. Once it had passed by the sirens shrieked, but the damage had been done and the plane was already gone. The strafing made us all quite jubilant, but we didn't dare show our feelings too much in that direction for we might find ourselves looking down the muzzle of one of those trusty rifles, and that we so well knew was a quick way to sudden death. No one was in any particular hurry to eliminate himself from the fold, even though he wasn't too fond of the surroundings.

Church services were held here on Sunday, just as they had been at the bases from whence we came. But there was a considerable difference, for now we had no chapel and no chaplains either. But we did have English Padres and they served the purpose well. As a matter of fact the Padres did an excellent job under the most trying of conditions and to them went the unselfish thanks of the thousands unto whom they ministered faithfully Sunday after Sunday. How or where they were captured I do not know. Perhaps they gave themselves up to the enemy, feeling that they would be able to do an untold amount of good in prison camps, where a chaplain is surely needed if anywhere. At least such would be my belief for if there is anywhere in the world where the soul needs ministering unto it is in prison camps where all looks the blackest and every minute one has the feeling that the world is plotting against you.

The services were held under the firmament unless it was too stormy, in which case they were held in one of the long narrow dark hallways of the barracks. But come rain, snow, sleet, hail, or fair weather, church was held, make no mistake about it. The weather made no difference. Catholic services were held in the morning between the hours of ten thirty and twelve, while the Protestant services were held in the afternoon between the hours of two thirty and four. The exact hour that they began depended upon what time the Padre arrived for the service, and of course his arrival was dependent upon how much the Germans cooperated in getting him from one compound to the other, which in some cases was quite good, while in others it was rather shameful. To aid in the singing we had a small pump organ, and also a few hymnals that had been sent to the camp, for this express purpose by the YMCA. The equipment was very limited and had to be taken care of judiciously for it had to last. Each Sunday it was moved from one compound to the other until all had had their respective services. Thus the food for the soul was supplied to the waiting thousands, just as Jesus fed the five thousand with 5 barley loaves and two fishes.

Our service was the last to be held today, so after its completion I went to the Padre, and asked him if I might take the organ to my room. He readily consented, with the proviso that I return it the following morning to Block eight where it was to be locked up in the general supply room. This I told him I would only be too glad to do, so with the aid of two of my companions we carried it back to the room placing it in one corner until after the evening meal had been completed at which time it was placed in the center of the room and a bench slid up to it. Now we were ready to go, if only we had a musician to play it, and that we had right in our own room, in the person of Ben Bower, a really fine piano player from Chicago, Illinois. He was very adept at the instrument for never having played one before and entertained the boys in the room, as well as the entire barracks for four or five hours by playing his vast repertoire of songs. It was a wonderful way to idle away a few hours, and so impressed were the boys with it that at times they would all break out and sing to his accompaniment. Thus a regular song fest was in session at various intervals. "Ben" was very obliging and played requests simply for the asking. It was a great morale builder and took our minds away from our present troubles, lifting them up into the lofts of the great beyond, swallowing us up entirely in the world of music and delight. As he played the different numbers it was interesting to note the reaction of the men to them, for it seemed everyone was recalling some pleasant incident that had happened when he heard it last. I remember quite distinctly my reaction when he played "Winter Wonderland." It brought to my mind the Junior Senior Prom at college, for it happened to be the theme song for that event. Tears came to my eyes, and I would have given almost anything just to be back there once more if but just for an instant, but such was not to be. My spirit and mind made the long journey, but my body was still very much locked up behind the stately barbed wire fences. At the close of the evening Ben played "Good Night Ladies" and so brought to a close a truly memorable evening. The actual value in dollars and cents of the music he so graciously supplied us with could never be determined. It was just one of those things that made an exceedingly dull life seem bearable. Despite the cold and uncomfortable bunks we slept well for the remainder of the night and for that super period of relaxation we could thank the musician and the music. They had given us temporary relaxation and relief such as we had never experienced before.

The last day of October was upon us. Already I had been a prisoner for nearly two months. My birthday anniversary had come and gone some days ago. Not even had I bothered to stop and recall the date. Would I spend another here? I hoped not but that was the best I could do for the present. I honestly doubted it but the best thing to do in a place such as this was to live from day to day and let the worries take care of themselves. For me to do otherwise was utterly useless for I could do very little to help matters.

After roll call our compound C.O. Spicer called us to his barracks to give a short talk. I do not remember his exact words, nor do I have access to them, much to my regret for I should like nothing better than to be able to quote him exactly. In effect he told us that there had been entirely too much fraternization with the guards, for visiting purposes only. He did not mind trading with them if we succeeded in taking advantage of them, but other than that we were to leave them strictly alone hereafter, and this was the reason he gave. A short time ago an allied prisoner, who was captured in Holland, after being forced to bail from his ship, entered this compound. When captured by the Germans, he was taken to one of the cities under their jurisdiction to headquarters. While enroute to those headquarters they passed a Holland mother with her small child in her arms. The mother had made the "V" sign with her fingers as he passed by and the guard shot both her and the child at that instant. These men are cold blooded murderers and I don't want you to be courting the good will of kindly relations of them. They are not worthy of our consideration. Remember we are still at war, they are your enemies and mine, so let us have no more to do with them than is absolutely necessary.

While he was giving this little speech there were several Germans standing in our midst taking it all in. He was well aware of that fact too, but he had spoken nothing but the truth, so should have been doing no one an injustice, but they did not feel quite that way about the situation. They decided that this was adverse publicity and the less we heard of such horrible truths the better. However, it was no news to any of us though for we had all seen just such things ourselves before arriving here. But in spite of that fact when he had finished a German officer and an enlisted man, who understood English, and had listened intently, came up and took the Colonel with them. He was put in the "Clink," and there would remain until he stood trial for his grievous crime of telling the truth. From his solitary cell he was taken to Stettin to stand trial. He was court martialed for "inciting a riot," and slandering the name of the good German people. After nearly three months had elapsed he was sentenced to death. German justice as the Nazi party dealt it out! We received word of the action on January 2, 1945. However, we were informed at the same time that it would not be carried out until the proper authorities in the United States had been notified. How long that would take was anyone's guess, but estimates ran up as high as three months. We all hoped it would take at least that long for if nothing else maybe the war would be over and thus save the life of a truly gallant, honest man. We could not bear the thought of an innocent man being shot for a crime he had not committed, but in our present predicament we were in no position to do anything about it. Guilty or not guilty, you try to convince the enemy when you find yourself on the "inside looking out." Their courts of Justice did not exactly deal in justice, but principally in politics. The Nazi, Gestapo and SS, were all ruthless murderers and their courts ran along much the same line.

Upon dismissal by the Colonel I started walking aimlessly around the compound, and as I had nothing urgent to do anyway, I felt I might just as well stop in and see some of my navigator classmates who had dropped in since my arrival at the camp. It was not the best place to visit, but then it was a very pleasant thought indeed that they too had survived, and made it to prison camp without too much bodily harm. After visiting with each of them for nearly an hour the noon hour rolled around so I returned to my own room to partake of the noon time snack. I had finished and just lain down in my "sack" when someone shouted out "showers up." What a scramble and shuffle of feet that brought about. The congestion in the rooms and halls was terrific, for everyone wanted to take a bath, and was running like mad to get his towel, and soap, with little or no regard for who might be in his path. I believe it was even worse then when they called "Red Cross up," at least equally as bad, for everyone wanted to make the first party, which consisted of forty men, no more, no less. If you did not make the first, and only a small portion of the men could, for there were more than 200 in the barracks, you would have to wait until they took another party, which at times would be in another 14 or 20 minutes, while at other times would not be until two weeks later. For that reason alone the rush to get into the first party is easily understandable. But to make it you would either have had to had some previous warning, or be a fleet foot. Either that or be hopelessly lost in the traffic jam at the door, and once you found yourself stranded in that position you might just as well turn around and go back to your room and try again the next time they called. The same mad scramble would take place all over again, and if you were one of the fortunate few you might make it. If not, you would just continue trying until either the fourth or fifth party rolled around. One of those you were sure to make for by that time most of the men would have had showers. many of the men, rather than make two or three futile attempts, waited until the past party thus eliminated all the wear and tear. I doubted the advisability of that action for too often you found yourself without a shower at all, and they were so rare that when you did have a chance to get one it was worth the extra effort expended to get in the first party.

There was an alternative to all this waiting and rushing though if you desired to take it. You could walk up to the washroom and take a cold bath under one of those liquid ice faucets if you felt so inclined, and could stand the shock of this freezing weather. It was not a very pleasant thought but it was much better than going dirty, and so was done by many of the men. The first time I saw one of them doing it I said that I could never do it, but I shall have to admit that I soon changed my way of thinking and it did not take long either, for to go two weeks without a bath, and often a month was unbearable. It was more than I could stand so I took intermittent baths at the washroom to supplement those given at the showers.

To begin with the shower room was not in our compound, and as in all cases when you leave your compound you must line up, be counted, recounted and miscounted, until finally they arrive at some figure and let you out of the gate. Forty was all that could be in a party, and if there were more the extras would have to return. If there were too few they would hold us all up until enough came to fill out the party. So after much standing and waiting we finally got to the showers, and once we arrived we wondered why we had been so eager, for the maximum time the water was permitted to run was three to five minutes. This hardly gave us time to get well soaped up, for two men had to use each shower head. However, it was much better than none at all. At times we did get more water, but it was only because they had bribed the Germans in charge with cigarettes for additional time under the showers. He would accept them and quite readily, if there were no superior officers around and he deemed it safe, otherwise he would turn a deaf ear to the plea. For once he were caught with the cigarettes, it would be him just like any other guard. They had a one way ticket to the "Clink" and the officer who found the cigarettes on him would have the smokes. There was a vast difference between the men working there, for some would take the risk quite gladly, while others would turn a deaf ear without even giving it any consideration.

The shower was over, so I dried myself off, put on my clothes and fell out in front of the building. Then came that same counting process again. Not once but four times to get back into my own compound. I sometimes wonder just what they would have done had some one disappeared enroute. According to all outward appearances they would not let you in unless the proper number was there whether they actually would have or not we never had the opportunity to find out, for there were always ample guards present to see that you did not get away.

This evening we were all patiently waiting for lights out time to arrive, so we could open our shutters and heckle the guards. We had given them no indication of what was going to happen, but rather let them believe that this would be just as any other night. They were surely going to be in for a surprise once the time came, and now it was not far off. In another fifteen minutes the time came, the lights went out, and we opened the shutters just as we always did at this time. But there was a decided difference, for instead of going to bed as per usual the men got out the small plastic flute and began to send code messages across the compound. As the camp was composed exclusively of airmen, we chose the International Morse code as a base, for we had all studied it during our training and so could all understand it. It was a great way to send messages back and forth after lights out, as contact by any other means was virtually impossible. You could hear the messages streaking back and forth, all over the area, and in most rooms there was a man taking them down as they came in, so the answer could be given. The German on guard duty, just knew that we must be up to something for this had never happened previously, so expected the worst. They were certain this was the signal for a mass break so doubled and even tripled their guard at some places, when actually all we were doing was annoying them. The search lights were going around like mad, and the dogs that had been turned loose in the compound were doing likewise, for every time a flute would sound from one window he would make his way to it, and no sooner had he arrived when another flute would sound from one of the windows in a far off corner. Away the dog would dash to that one. It was an endless and fruitless journey for by the time he got halfway across the compound two more would sound off simultaneously. All of which made the dog very angry and even more confused, and us very very happy for we had succeeded in annoying them beyond all measure. You can readily imagine just how happy those guards were that had to get up in the middle of the night, and go back on duty, from which they had just been relieved. The message sending went on for hours and by the time that it was over the news that had been made available to us in the daytime by the guards and various other sources had been disseminated all over the camp, even to the men in solitary confinement. Formerly they had been shut out entirely, but now with the toy flutes that need no longer be the case. Yes the toy flutes that made their way to the camp came in mighty handy and did aid materially in sending wireless messages from one compound to the other, as well as to the cells. The men in the cells could not answer, but nevertheless they knew we were thinking of them and had not forgotten to heckle the guards in their absence.

Ah! You say, but the Germans know the Morse Code too. To which I would reply, yes, perhaps they did, but what percentage of them did? What would you say was the average number who could understand it? And how did they know which one to be listening to, for we had more than one going at a time and it was only a certain pitch that counted. All the rest was just so much "static" thrown into confuse them. I am a bit afraid they never did solve the problem entirely, at least such would be my guess, for it is very unlikely that they would have a bunch of professional code crackers as guards at a prison camp.

Now that we had had our fun we retired and slept over our most recent feat of devilment, which as you probably know made us all very happy, at least for the moment. And after all any little cheer that could be brought to the group, such as that, helped to make a bad situation a little brighter, for without those moments, camp would have been most unbearable. It would probably have driven most of the men insane or prompted them to commit suicide, both of which happened anyway, but not to the degree it would have, had we had no comeback on the Germans at all.

And so life went on from day to day with little or no change, and nothing exciting happening, except in rare instances. To take the camp on a day to day basis from here on out would prove very dull reading, for it would amount to nothing but worry about food and fuel, both of which were to gradually get worse up to the point where it was almost unbearable.

So from here on with your most gracious permission I shall elaborate only on the main chain of events as they took place. The information will all be taken from my personal diary, and is true and accurate to the best of my knowledge.

On November 7th, 1944 we were x-rayed for T.B. at the expense of the American Red Cross, that is, those of us who wanted to be. The apparatus was all under German control and supervision, so for results we had to rely on their statements. It was entirely on a voluntary basis, but as there was nothing to lose, I decided that it would be best to have a check and see if it had developed. And if so to what extent. We understood that we were to be repatriated if there were any signs of it, but whether that happened to anyone or not I am not in a position to say, for as far as I know there were no cases, however I did not check into it so thoroughly for I felt sure that if I had it they could tell me, and if not, why worry about it. Worry in this camp just hastened the time when you would lose your mind entirely, and I was in no hurry to lose mine for I wanted to get out of here with all the faculties with which I had entered it, and so kept myself busy.

My chief pastime was working on tin, for it was the most abundant material available, and had many uses to which it could be put. While there, I made many pans, a cracker grinder which I have already mentioned, a complete set of dominoes, each of which contain the autograph of some famous person in prison camp, a rule and a novelty lamp. The dominoes took nearly two months to complete and the lamp took even more than that considering the time spent in construction, detail and actual cutting and assembling. Besides this hobby I also did fancy lettering, making signs for the office with slogans such as, "I Complained when I had no shoes, until I met a man who had no feet." Still other lettering was done in my own small log book, which contained memorials to the boys on my crew, poems written in prison camp, dedications to the Generals of the Armies in the Field, and excerpts from letters received in prison camp. My diary was kept

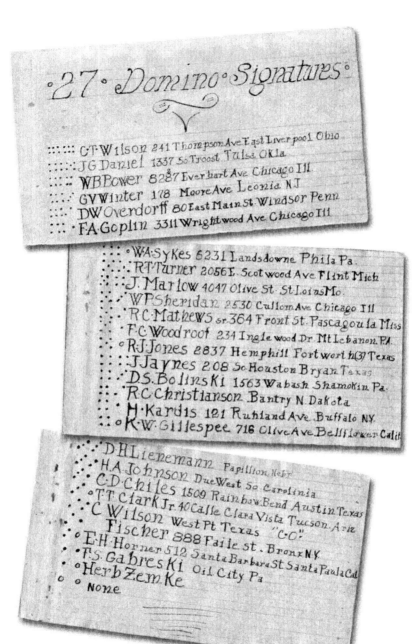

°27° Domino° Signatures°

CT Wilson 241 Thompson Ave East Liverpool Ohio
JG Daniel 1337 So Troost Tulsa Okla
WB Bower 8287 Everhart Ave Chicago Ill
GV Winter 178 Moore Ave Leonia NJ
DW Overdorff 80 East Main St Windsor Penn
FA Goplin 3311 Wrightwood Ave Chicago Ill

WA Sykes 5231 Landsdowne Phila Pa.
RT Turner 2056 L Scotwood Ave Flint Mich
J. Marlow 4047 Olive St St Louis Mo.
WP Sheridan 2530 Cullom Ave Chicago Ill
RC Mathews sr 364 Front St Pascagoula Miss
FC Woodroof 234 Inglewood Dr Mt Lebanon PA.
RJ Jones 2837 Hemphill Fort worth (3) Texas
J Jaynes 208 So Houston Bryan Texas
DS Bolinski 1563 Wabash Shamokin Pa.
RC Christianson Bantry N Dakota
H Kardis 121 Ruhland Ave Buffalo NY.
KW Gillespee 716 Olive Ave Bellflower Calif

DH Lienemann Papillion Nebr
HA Johnson DueWest So Carolina
CD Chiles 1509 Rainbow Bend Austin Texas
TT Clark Jr 40 Calle Clara Vista Tucson Ariz
C Wilson West Pt Texas "C-O"
Fischer 888 Faile st. Bronx NY.
EH Horner 512 Santa Barbara St Santa Paula Cal
FS Gabreski Oil City Pa
Herb Zemke
None

Names of fellow POW's included inside the donimo set.

in the same fashion. That portion of it dating from September 1944 to February 1, 1945 was all kept on soap wrapper that had been carefully removed from the bars of soap contained in Red Cross parcels for that was the only paper available at the time. On the latter date I received a composition book through the courtesy of the international YMCA and so started using it.

As the days went by eating became slimmer and slimmer, but soon we were to be filled at least once more for the cook had been laying back a little each day, saving slowly but surely for the approaching Thanksgiving holiday. We celebrated this festival on the 30th day of November for we had no Christmas shopping to do anyway, and ate like kings. As to quantity I can truthfully say the day ended with every one of us comfortably full. However, to obtain that feeling for just one day, necessitated saving for a whole month and going without many of the things we would have liked but were willing to sacrifice for one final splurge and make Thanksgiving more evident than it would have been without the additional quantity of food.

During the afternoon divine services were held just as they had been on Sundays, but there was a striking difference, considering attendance anyway, for the area was full of men. Every one had taken this opportunity to come and thank the most good and gracious Lord for his most recent delivery from what seemed at the time inescapable death.

It turned out that we had been more fortunate and survived; just how, or why, this was accomplished some of us still had not figured out, but the fact remained that we were very much alive and here. True enough, prison camp was not the best place in the world to be, quite the contrary in fact, but then it was a much better fate than many of our very best friends had suffered, literally thousands of whom lay strewn from border to border today in Germany proper. What a thought to harbor, but we knew it to be true for many of us had seen them go to their deaths. We only hoped that they had received a decent burial, and more than that we were unable to do for the present. The Lord had been most gracious to us and had held out His guiding and protecting hand from that day onward, and we had not forgotten, nor did we want to. This truth had left an indelible print in our minds, never to be removed, not even by the severest storm that might come our way. What we wanted most of all was for this horrible war to be brought to an end so that we might be taken from this camp back to our loved ones in the States, but that was asking for a lot as the picture stood now.

The news was depressing, so depressing in fact we would have done well to have had none at all. "Aachan was rocking." "Aachan had been rocking" for some time, but somehow Aachen just would not fall. It was one of those inexplicable things. We could not understand how they could hold out under the pressure that was undoubtedly being put on them, but in spite of that, somehow the breakthrough just would just not come. The battle had dragged itself into a stalemate, all of which made us none too happy, for we were well aware that it was forestalling the final day, thus lengthening the time we would be required to stay. We could put up with it, yes, for there was nothing else to do—we would not even be consulted in the matter. Nevertheless we did not exactly relish the idea, and for that you could not exactly blame us. Aachen finally fell sometime in the early part of December, but that is as far as the Allies got for they were again halted just on the outside of the city itself, and there the line remained steadfast until the great German winter offensive began under the able guidance of field Marshall Von Rundsteadt. His push as you will probably remember started around the 19th of December, and you can be sure they lost no time telling us about it. Whether they ever got in as far as their reports indicated is questionable, but they had at least done a good job of scaring us, and had postponed the end of the war even further.

Every time that we were near the breaking point, as far as morale was concerned, something would inevitably turn up to release that strain, and thus take our minds from our ever present troubles, of which it seemed we had way more than our share. December 6 was just such a day, and the treat was the showing of the film "Spring Parade" featuring Deana Durbin. It had been sent in by the YMCA or the American Red Cross as had the small projector and sound devices. Many of us had seen the film some time previously, but as we had seen no movies for some time, and were unlikely to see any in the very near future we went again. The showing took several hours and was thoroughly enjoyed by everyone present. It was indeed wonderful to think that even here in the midst of all our trials and woes we could enjoy an American film, sound track and all. The girls who acted in that picture brought tears to many of the men's eyes as they sat there closely watching the proceedings and singing the lovely songs so beautifully portrayed. The setting and scenery was more than some of the prisoners could bear, for no doubt they were drawing correlations between what was transpiring on the screen and what had occurred while free men and able to be with their loved ones, now left behind. It reminded us even more of those wonderful United States, we had lost all contact with, never to see again until the end of the war. When that would be was anyone's guess, we were not too optimistic, but had given up hopes of being home by Easter. We waited, even though it was not too patiently.

December the 9th as I was walking around the compound, doing nothing much in particular except getting a breath of fresh air, I walked up to the bulletin board on block five and looked over the list of the latest men who had been shipped into our camp. I hastily scanned it, to see if there might be someone I knew, and there to my utter amazement, was the name of Wayne H. Burhmann. Could it be the Wayne Burhmann, "Red," I had gone to college with? The same one that I had gone into the army with? It did not seem likely for the last I had heard of him he was in the States. I checked his serial number, then compared it with mine. If that was any indication it could be for we had both gotten our commissions about the same time. Still it seemed a bit far-fetched to believe, but there was only one way to find out! I went to the American C.O. room, explained to him the circumstances, and asked for permission to visit North III Compound, in which the bulletin said he was located. "Sorry you can not go today, but maybe we can slip you through tomorrow on some detail," said the Colonel. So I gave him my name, and immediately after roll call the following morning went to the office to see if I had made it. My anxiety was killing me. I found upon arrival that I had. What a break, oh happy day, now if it was the "Red" this would be some reunion and would he ever be surprised to see me! I walked into his barracks and there was "Red" coming down the hall, for it happened it was "Goon Guard." To say that he was startled would be a gross understatement. His expression indicated he could not believe his eyes and rightly so, for he had no way of knowing that I was around so never once expected to see me. "What a small world this is," I said to him.

"Don, well of all people, where the heck did you come from?"

"Just dropped over to see you Red, I have taken up residence over in North II some time ago, three months ago to be exact."

"Well, how the dickens did you get over here?"

"There's angles my boy, if you know the right people. I did not know them with I first came in either, but I have made it my business to get acquainted. Seriously Red, I got over here on a hoax, and the less said about the matter the better."

"Why the last time I saw you was at Lincoln, Nebraska."

"That's right, remember we drove to Omaha to see a show just the night before I shipped out?"

"As I live and breathe I still find trouble believing what I see."

"Yep, it's me alright, and very much alive too."

The more we discussed the situation the more unbelievable it became. To think that 18 of us had been taken from college at the same time and two of those 18 should end up in the same prison camp. It was utterly fantastic, for there were 23 or more camps in Germany and the chances of getting shot down and into the same camp were so minute they did not even warrant any consideration, but somehow it had happened. Fate must have had a holiday.

It was a wonderful reunion for both of us, for I dare say we never once expected to meet in the heart of Germany, especially under such conditions. But we both found out it is not exactly what you think or expect, rather what actually happens that counts. To say that I would prefer to meet my friends elsewhere under different circumstances would be a gross understatement, however I was plenty glad to see "Red" for at least it meant that he had gotten out alive and had arrived here without suffering too much additional bodily harm. His head was all bandaged up and he looked as though he had taken a good beating, but aside from that was still mobile, which in itself was much to be thankful for. He told me that he knew "Dick Pascal" was down, but he was not sure just what camp he was being sent to. Dick was another of the original 18 but never did arrive at Barth. Still another of our classmates, Willard Hunzeker had finished his missions and was back visiting Peru State Teachers College telling about his experiences, before going back for more duty. This indeed will give you some idea of just how we acquired our information in prison camps. We always got it from the latest recruits. It might have been a bit old, but at least we had not heard of it before, so it was news to us. After a most enjoyable visit I returned to my own compound and was greatly relieved for my curiosity had been satisfied. The war news that he had imparted to me was everything but bright, so black in fact that I did not even pay much attention to it. I would just as soon not know what was going on, when it hit such a low ebb. Meeting Wayne was truly one of the highlights of my camp career, and one that I shall never forget.

As we made our way out to roll call on December the 19th, 1944, we could not help noticing the haughty attitude of the Germans. Something had surely gone in their favor, this much was evident for they had little or no consideration for anyone. We wondered just what it was that was making them feel so "cocky" but we did not have to wonder long, for they told us that Von Rundsteadt had started a huge German winter offensive, and now they were going to push our troops way back to the coast, if not into the English Channel and North Sea. Of course no one believed that they would succeed in getting us shoved back that far but from all indications they must have managed to do quite a bit of pushing or had certainly caught us unaware just below Aachan. Forty miles deep and 25 miles wide, and way over into Belgium was no laughing matter. Apparently our lines had been completely shattered and it was just a matter of time until they got spread out all over Belgium and France again. Paris by Christmas was their byword, and if one was to believe them, they would most assuredly make it. I rather doubted it, but with nothing but their version of the news I could not be at all sure of my convictions. After a time they get you so indoctrinated with their propaganda, that you begin to believe it, even though you know right well that 90% of it is lies. But it seems if you hear those same lies often enough they will begin to register. Try as we would to convince ourselves, it just could not be done, for apparently it was true, at least no news was forthcoming that indicated any falsehoods in their statements. Every time they took another square foot they would be sure to let us know about it, throwing in a couple of extra feet for good measure, and to make the figure more impressive. But the fact remained that even if we cut their figures in two they were still doing a remarkable job. Such a thing had not happened to the Germans for some time, and they were getting to the point where you could not reach them with a ten foot pole. They were the victors, they were the ones who were gaining ground, they were going to win the war, and we would find ourselves rebuilding all the cities that we had blown to bits. Yes, they told us that once this war was over we would be taken to all the cities we had so unmercifully bombed and could start putting the buildings back as they were before the war. A very pleasant thought, for some of those cities were in terrible shambles, and to rebuild them would take ages. With all this running through my mind, I began to recall once more the many things that I had seen on that train trip across Germany. Inside of Germany itself I saw few if any fortifications, so once our troop got into it there would be little to stop them, but first they must get through the Siegfried, and across the Rhine, both of which they were working on feverishly, at the time I was in the area. No doubt they intended to throw in everything they had there and try to stem the tide. If that failed they stood to lose everything. Here they were going to make their do or die attempt. As it looked right now our troops were having no success getting through either of the strongholds. As a matter of fact everything had been brought to a standstill and the Germans had succeeded in giving us a severe setback to boot. We had one other though on which we relied quite heavily and that was the memory of men and boys we had seen going to the front. They were already sending men of 50, 60 or over at the time I came into camp, and surely they could not stand up under modern mechanized battle conditions for long. They were also sending young boys of fourteen to sixteen, but I learned from one of the guards that these were mostly to be used as suicide squads, so they would in all possibility be very short lived. The question was how much damage would they be able to inflict before they put themselves out of misery. To what extent had they been used on the most recent breakthrough? All questions with no answers readily available. We were in position to do anything but guess. Assuming for awhile that everything they told us about the offensive was true, then surely they must have used a goodly number. Perhaps now they had done their damage and it would only be a matter of days until they were pushed back. There could even be one more solution, and I kept wondering whether this was not it. As a matter of fact I hoped it was. Perhaps the Americans had made a weak spot in their lines intentionally for the express purpose of drawing the Germans into a pocket. Once they got a goodly number in there, they would cut them off from their own supply lines and methodically annihilate them. It could be done and would have been very good tactics, for it would have eliminated the necessity of going after them, but had it been figured out this way? That was just another thing that we did not know. Soon you will come to the conclusion—we did not know anything. Oh, how right you are, too.

We were in the depths of despair. The news was terrible, the food was worse, and fuel was at a premium. To top it off with Christmas just 6 days away we did not know for sure which way to turn or just what to do. So, rather than give it any further thought, skipped the matter entirely and tried as best we could to prepare for the approaching holidays, thus making the very best of a bad situation, which after all would be just what our parents and loved ones at home would want us to, under the prevailing circumstances. The change of mind must have done some good for when the 22nd day of December rolled around, we had aid in the form of food. What a substantial boost that gave to our wavering, tottering morale. It was much more than we could ever have hoped for. What should it be but American Red Cross Prisoner of War CHRISTMAS parcels. An oasis in the midst of this dearth. The number that had arrived would not permit a parcel to be issued to each man, individually, but necessitate issuing four parcels to five men. They then would split the contents as best they could, so each would have a fine Christmas dinner. This was not too bad, as a matter of fact it was much better than we had ever dreamed possible just a few short days before. Again a light had shone on the horizon, to make what was going to be one of the blackest of Christmases a bit brighter. I shall now list for you the complete contents of the parcel so you too will have some idea just how we dined on Christmas Day 1944.

3 pkgs. cigarettes
1 pkg. smoking tobacco
1 pipe
1 washcloth
2 pictures (American scenes)
1 lb. plum pudding
12 oz. turkey (boned meat)
4 oz. sausages
6 oz. strawberry jam
12 oz. assorted candy
3 oz. deviled ham
4 oz. cheddar cheese
12 oz. mixed nuts
12 bouillon cubes
2 fruit bars
6 oz. honey
2 – 8 oz. tea
1 pack playing cards
4 packages chewing gum
2 – ¾ oz. butter
1 box (games assorted)

By studying the list carefully you can see with little or no trouble at all that irrespective of how dismal a situation may look or may actually be, there is always a little good cheer comes along to alleviate an otherwise unbearable situation. Christmas did just that.

At roll call Christmas morning, the members of my room, and those of the room across the hall put on a little stunt for the rest of the compound. With the aid of several of my roommates I had cut out the letters "Merry Christmas Block 3," and these we had pinned on to the men that were to stand in the front rank. The block captain had dressed up the formation in four ranks and when this was completed the men with their letters came out of the barracks, ran around the formation and walked down to their proper positions along the front, forming the fifth rank. Once they were lined up a big round of applause and many cheers came from the rest of the compound, so more happiness had been spread in our midst. When they finished counting our formation the letters were changed to read "Come on Ike." What this did you can readily imagine. It veritably brought down the house, much to the displeasure of the Germans. However, they did not worry about it much for their success was still apparently going forward unhampered.

With roll call over we returned to our barracks, and ate breakfast, and this time it was really breakfast too, not just a thin slice or two of bread as it had been. We would at least eat today, whether we would tomorrow or not was debatable, and at the time was given no concern either. During the day everyone again attended the service of their choice and today much like Thanksgiving, the services were unusually well attended. Everyone rejoiced as he harkened back once more to those days just some one thousand nine hundred and forty four years ago, when some one else, namely Joseph, was having trouble too, so much in fact that he could not find a place for his wife, Mary, to lay her head, and so after many trials and failures was forced as a last resort to take a lowly manger in a stable at Bethlehem. This then was to be the birthplace of the infant "Jesus, our Savior and Redeemer." It was He who had so graciously saved us from what was so nearly the end, and would have been had He not interceded and extended to us His assistance. I often wondered just why He saved us, what He had in mind for us to do, once this war ended, and we were released from this prison camp? Why did He save us and permit so many others to go to their death? It gave us plenty to think about. What grounds did we have for complaint? In reality none. We should indeed be thankful to be alive and well. Even though ours was a far cry from what we were used to, and even farther from what we would have liked for the occasion, it could quite easily have been much worse.

By noon the sky had about sixty percent coverage of Alto Cumulus clouds and by the time nightfall drew upon us it had turned to a leaden gray. Morale here follows the condition of the sky almost to a "T" for we realized that in bad weather our ground troops can not have the full support of the Air Corps and when that is not possible we know their job is much more difficult and costly in life and materials than would it be should good flying weather prevail.

With Christmas over I began preparations for the new year. A roll call stunt would be good, but what would I do this time that was different from last to create a good laugh, and thus start the day out right? Just the words "Happy New Year" in themselves would not be enough, for without a doubt the rest of the compound would expect that now, as a follow up of the Christmas antic. It would have to be that plus something else to give it that added zest that "oomph" so to speak. The idea accepted must be in line with the materials at hand too, and that was the big problem. Materials were so scarce, as a matter of fact every time we made something it was more or less on the policy of "Robbing Peter to Pay Paul." If we needed a few nails we would take them from the barracks or in the latrine. If we needed scraps of wood they would be torn from the attic. Eventually the building would fall down due to lack of materials and braces, but we hoped that we would not stay that long. I asked several of my roommates what they thought, and after many suggestions finally took the one given by Lt. Wilson. Portray the old year 1944 and the New Year 1945. It sounded feasible, if we could get the men in the barracks who were best suited for the parts to do it. If they would accept, then I would go ahead with the work, otherwise not. So we went down to see Lt. Charles Bain, a short good natured fellow from Bloomington, Illinois, in room three, presented the problem to him and asked him if we could have his cooperation in the matter. Would he be the infant 1945? The answer was yes, so half of the battle was won. We told him on leaving that we would like to keep it as quiet as possible until that day, for we did not want to be "scooped." He promised faithfully to keep the secret. We then went to room ten to see "Snake" a tall lanky fellow to ask him if he would be Old decrepit 1944. He, too, readily assented, so we were all fixed, in regard to the men for the parts anyway. The next thing on the program was to assemble the necessary equipment for the men, and that would necessitate a lot of ingenuity.

I drew up the scythe on cardboard, and then with the invaluable aid of "Scratch" Overdorff, cut it out. We made about six thickness, and wired it together as best we could using holes that had been punched into the cardboard to facilitate the process After that I cut the blade for the scythe from a single rigid piece of cardboard we had, and fastened it on. Now the only thing lacking was the hand grips and they were made from scraps of wood gathered in the aforementioned manner. Aside from the scythe 1944 must have an old lantern, which was made by "Al" Thomas of room nine, a long flowing gown, for which a sheet would do, a long silvery chain wrapped about his waist, whiskers, and a 1944 ribbon flowing from his chest. The chain was made by Lt. Wilson from cigarette cellophane wrappers, while I made the whiskers and the flowing ribbon. The whiskers proved to be quite a problem, but after much persuasion I managed to talk one of the guards out of some spun glass for the purpose, then went back to my barracks and put the proper backing under it, so it might be attached to the face. The flowing 1944 ribbon was made of scraps of paper I had received from the office, as was the 1945 ribbon worn by "Charles" Old year was all set to go. Now for the new year and this left many problems yet unsolved, but after due consideration and much planning we managed to make a reasonably accurate facsimile of a silk topper, from still blank paper and cardboard and a small sporty cane. For diapers we used a bath towel, and secured it in place with a large safety pin that had been made expressly for the purpose by the men in room nine. It was about sixteen inches long and quite visible to the group when it finally made its appearance. Now there was but one remaining hitch.

Now to make it look as though he were in his bare skin, but yet would not be, for it was too cold for that. Two or three pairs of long underwear would do the trick, if I could but find them. I had one pair in my kit, Charles had one, which made two, so one more was all that was needed. After a little searching I found it, and with that the problems were solved. Now I was all set to again give the boys a little boost in morale, which by this time was badly needed, for it seemed nothing would stop the German offensive, and as a result the men were growing more despondent every day.

Something had to be done, and with the arrival of New Years Day, we dressed up the two "victims," and after everyone else had fallen out for roll call and were in their proper positions, we let them come running from the barracks, the infant 1945 chasing old and gray 1944. It was quite a spectacle as they made their way between the various groups, and the stunt was received with much applause, as well as with a good many hearty laughs. To add to the hilarity it was icy underfoot and this of course added to the proceedings for it was inevitable that they fall with the speed they were traveling. After they had gone around and between all the blocks so everyone could see them they returned to our block area, put on their overcoats and lined up for the counting which was ready to take place. Even the Germans had gotten a big kick out of the proceedings for when they came to the man who had portrayed 1944, they asked him if he wanted to be counted too. To which he naturally replied yes. It was all very inspiring and well worth the work that it had taken to bring it into being. At least everyone was happy for the moment and had smiled because he could not resist, rather than being forced to. Spontaneous laughter quenched many ills, and made the whole atmosphere of the camp brighter. It gave you something to think about during the remainder of the day, too, and every time you would recall the incident you could smile again.

But all this smiling was of very short duration for on January 2, as you will remember my telling you, we received the news that Colonel Spicer had been sentenced to death. It was a terrific jolt, for we all loved the man very dearly and honestly felt that he had been dealt with unjustly. There was but one big hurdle confronting us, how to get help for the man, and that one was so big we could not begin to surmount it. We did the only thing we could under the circumstances. We prayed more fervently than ever that this war be brought to a close and thus spare his life. If that failed, our cause was lost. The more we thought about the unjustness of the sentence the more bitter we became. However, in due time our reasoning returned to normal. There was but one thing to do. Wait and see what the final outcome would be, but never forget to pray. Everyone was more or less uneasy about that sentence though and evidences of attempting to escape were being formulated all over the camp. The men had definitely not taken the sentence lying down. Should this war last past the spring season we meant to get out if at all possible. Actions indicated that the various projects were going full speed ahead, some still in the planning stage, while still others were in the actual process of construction. Tunnels were in all stages of completion, and one compound had as many as 52 different ones started, however they were all found by the Germans in time. It was impossible for us to dig any deeper than four or five feet before starting for the fence because of the water level. This was probably the worst hindrance, for it permitted the Germans to listen to our digging with the seismographs they had hidden in various parts of the camp. They would sit and listen to us work and every time a tunnel came near the fence they would come in and close it up. When they discovered number 52 they put up this sign:

Roses are red, violets are blue
This is the end, of tunnel "52"

That they have a sense of humor cannot be denied, that is as long as they are on the winning side, but when they happen to have the back seat it does not work quite that way. Then it is a different story entirely. There is another instance of tunnel digging that to me was always very interesting, and I shall pass it on to you to enjoy, too. It seems that the Germans were always finding the tunnels anyway, regardless of how well the entrance was hidden, so one of the boys conceived the idea of starting one just a little way from the barracks, which he did. But about a month before they actually began work on the project they gathered a few boards from various and sundry places and threw them haphazardly on a pile where the entrance was to be. This done they made a sign post labeled it "Ye Ole Tunnel" and placed it in the very center of the heap. Thus it remained untouched by human hands for several weeks, no one disturbing it whatsoever, except to walk over it, as though it had no significance at all. When work on the tunnel once began they were always very careful that they would not be seen by any of the Germans, then when they finished for the night, they would throw the boards haphazardly over the top and replace the sign. The Germans saw the sign many times, for that is exactly why it was put there, but thought it was just a prank and were not going to be embarrassed by taking a look, especially while they could be seen. As a result they never did look until the tunnel was almost completed, when one day their curiosity got the better of them and they removed the sign and boards, and much to their amazement, and I might add to their embarrassment they did find a tunnel. They lost no time in filling it, but their faces were surely red for having missed a well-labeled tunnel for such a long period of time. They waited nearly too long to investigate that one.

You may gather from this that "via the tunnel" was the only method used in attempted escapes, but there is where you are very wrong indeed for we tried other methods, some of which were successful others of course were not. Another one of the unsuccessful methods used was the box kite. The boys built a small kite first just as a test model and then each succeeding day would build a larger one, until finally they had one that would lift sixty pounds. At this point the Germans discovered what they were up to and banned kite building for the duration. Just another dream that had been squelched in its infancy and while only half way to its goal, but soon someone would come forth with another bright idea of how it might be accomplished, so one lost any sleep over the ordeal. It was more or less of a race to see whether we could outwit our captors. Generally speaking we failed but we kept on trying in spite of it, and every once in awhile a successful method would be discovered.

Food was getting scarcer, but with the turn of events on the Russian front as of January 14, at least we had good news. The Russians had begun a big offensive in South Poland, using five complete armies as a spearhead. This we hoped fervently would be the beginning of the end, for our fuel situation was getting critical too. We had only enough to keep our fire burning about five hours a day. All the rest of the time the room was without heat of any kind, and being nearly 60 degrees north as we were, it was indeed uncomfortable. Such a winter I never, never want to see or go through again. To supplement our meager fuel ration we stole logs from the "sump," near our barracks. From the stagnant frozen mess we gathered the logs, took them to our room via the window after dark, and sawed them up for the stove. They were about eight to ten inches in diameter, and we sawed them into chunks ten inches long after which they were split with a table knife if you can imagine such a thing, for we had no other means of getting the job done. It would take hours to get even one piece cut off, but each chunk helped, and it kept you warm while you were working, so two goals were achieved with but a single stroke. I shall have to admit that the wood did burn up much faster than we were able to cut it into lengths, but it was a valuable supplement to our slim coal ration. It would provide a quick hot fire too, if such were ever necessary.

The news continued to be good as far as the Russian advances were concerned and by the twenty seventh of January they were 90 miles from Berlin, at least so our reports led us to believe. It seemed almost impossible that they could move so many hundreds of miles without stopping, but apparently they were doing it for Warsaw had fallen and the whole south end of their line just kept right on coming. There was no stopping to them and for that we were very happy, for if events continued in the present trend we would be free men in another 15 days. But somehow they failed to maintain that pace, even though the thirty first of January did find them lined up along the Oder River, 35 miles from Berlin and about that many miles from Stettin. Little did we know or ever once guess that those positions would remain nearly steadfast for the next two and one half months while they consolidated their gains and cleaned up isolated areas, but that is precisely what happened.

With the start of the Russian campaign many of the Germans who had moved into that area during the German occupation had to evacuate leaving everything behind. To supply these people with clothing the Germans had a salvage drive, but I would be led to believe that they did not fare too well, for on the 30th day of January they gave an order that all clothes in excess of one complete uniform in the possession of any prisoner would be confiscated and collected on February the third. What they were going to do with the clothes they did not say neither did they say where they had gotten the authority to take clothes from us that were a gift from our own American Red Cross. We challenged their right to make such a move, but as we had nothing to back it up with soon lost the argument. But we did not lose the clothes. They had made a gross blunder in giving us four day's notice, for when we found that they could not be talked out of it, the clothes were hidden. Every last stitch of it disappeared until the "heat" was off. We did not intend to alleviate the suffering that any German civilian might be undergoing for we honestly felt that if they became embittered toward their own government they might do something to stop this war, so we acted accordingly. After all, we were not exactly happy with our surroundings either and would gladly have gone back to the United States if they would permit us to do so. Which, needless to say, they would not.

Fifteen hundred prisoners of war arrived on January 30th too, all of whom had been evacuated from their camp ahead of the Russian onslaught. Why they did not permit them to remain in their camp and fall into the hands of the Russians, thus remove from their own shoulders lots of work, and lighten their guard burden I do not know. Perhaps it was because they felt that it would be better if the truth about what transpired in the German prison camps were not yet known, for the reprisal carried out by the Allies might be nothing short of terrific. I can see their point if that was their object, otherwise I should say they made a very foolish mistake.

The dawn of a new day, February 1st, and what a pleasant surprise I received. A note from a man in North III Compound reading thus:

"I sent your pictures home and heard from your Mother. She knows you are a P.O.W. What happened to the rest of your crew? Try to get over here. I'm in Block 9, Room 11, John H. Peters N-3."

The first news that I had from home and what a relief it was for now at least I had the assurance that they knew I was alive and a P.O.W. The whole affair was a miraculous coincidence, for it happened that J. H. Peters was the navigator on the other crew, which lived in the same hut that I did while based back in England. He was gone on flak leave the day I was shot down, but upon returning found some of my belongings that the squadron had failed to pick up. He wrapped them up and mailed them to my Mother, and she in turn wrote him thanking him for what he had done. Then along came January, and he was shot down too, and as fate would have it, was sent to the same prison camp that I was in. So he had delivered the message in person, which was a very pleasant surprise and brought me much relief. Whether or not she was getting any of my messages sent from prison camp I did not know for she had only mentioned that they had been notified by the War Department of my capture and imprisonment. But the point was she knew, and could rest somewhat easier too. I did get over to see him about a week later and we talked over what had transpired back at the base since my departure and I also enlightened him as to what had happened to the remainder of the crew. This was quite a blow to him, but he said later that he rather expected as much for the report had come back that the ship had exploded and there were no chutes visible. This in itself left little room for hope.

The war news was bad. Both fronts had ceased all forward movement, and to make matters even worse we were thirsty. The water had been turned off, and we had no place to get a drink. For two whole days this went on, and had it not been for the snow we were able to gather up the first day and melt giving each man a cup of water, I am not so sure how we would have survived. The second day there was no snow, so we did without entirely. We tried the faucets, but not a drip was forthcoming. We must go thirsty. Had it gone on a third day I am not at all sure what we might have resorted to. As I saw it there was but one move to make, and that was to take ice from the sump, filthy as it was, boil it thoroughly and then drink just enough to tide us over. Not a very pleasant thought, but when it comes to giving up life itself, or going on living, you don't let such thoughts deter you. You shut your eyes and use the last resort. It so happened we did not have to, for the next morning it was turned on.

February 5, 1945. Fuel ration cut 10 lumps, which means a cold room most of the time from now on. May cut down and eat twice a day to stretch our limited food supply. We don't live we just exist.

February 13, 1945. Food shortage here in force, but the Lord will provide for He always had thus far.

February 15, 1945. Never has the pantry been so S-L-I-M.

February 22, 1945. The pangs of hunger are really here now. Some eats, but very, very little.

The month of February, as you have noticed from reading the above excerpts from my diary, was one of the most trying in our entire stay, with the exception of March, which was soon to follow. The food rations became slimmer and slimmer and the coal ration was cut almost weekly meaning both smaller quantities of food and less heat. And we in the middle of winter, with very few clothes, still less bedding, trying to combat the elements. It just did not make sense, but make sense or not it was happening and everyone was going even more hungry and getting even colder than they had in the past. What prevented an epidemic from breaking out is very hard to say, but I will frankly admit that it was not the German's fault that such did not occur, but more than likely the good and gracious hand of the Lord, who did not see fit for such a thing to happen now that apparently everything else had gone wrong. Every day you could see men visit the incinerators, grub out half rotten rutabagas, take them to their rooms and eat them. Personally I can not honestly say that I was above such a thing, for I did it myself, and felt that "Pride must go before destruction" and so it went. I gathered the potato peelings that had been there for probably two months, took them to my room, cleaned them as best I could and cooked potato soup. Many of the other fellows did the same. It was mostly skins, yes, but it did fill a very empty space in my stomach. Then, too, I gathered some of the rutabagas and after removing the more badly rotten areas, ate them. Sometimes singly and then again in combination with my potato peelings. To make a bad situation even worse they gave us moldy bread to eat, but that did not deter us, for we ate it anyway, first however, it was toasted as best it could be by putting it on top of the stove and burning it thoroughly.

But these were by no means the only things eaten during this period. Not by any chance of the imagination. Rather they were only the beginning. The boys would catch moles, birds in improvised traps made of sticks, and even fish worms were dug up when the ground was not frozen too hard and fired them for a repast. Not exactly what we had been accustomed to eating, far less from what we enjoyed, but right then it tasted pretty good, for at least it was food. We also had three cats that frequented the compound.

Well, they came in once too often and lost out in the skirmish for they found their hides on someone's wall and their meat in the skillet. They all disappeared in one night never to return again. All this just to get the necessary stamina so that we might carry on, and finally get home. Soon the month of February had slipped by and we hoped that March would surely be better but much to our disappointment the situation grew worse from day to day. The only thing that we had to cling to at all was the news that managed to get to us, for it seemed the Russians were clearing one city after another, and the Americans, too, were again pushing at the gates of the powerful Siegfried line. Almost daily the names of cities would come in that the Americans were in the process of taking cities that we had bombed while still free men. As we knew the exact location it gave us a pretty accurate picture of where the fighting was taking place. March the third was the day that they were supposedly fighting in the suburbs of Düsseldorf. This brought to mind the day I had flown thirty miles up the Ruhr River valley, seven months ago, just to bomb that city. Finally it was getting its "Coup de Grace." They came very near getting me on that raid, but as fortune would have it we got back. The Ruhr valley was not exactly the best place in the world to fly, that is if you valued your life. As a matter of fact it was considered to be one of the most heavily gunned areas in the world for this was the heart of the great German war industry, and from this area came a large percentage of all the coal and fighting equipment.

Things were so bad in March that we actually had to cut cards to see just who would get first, second, third, fourth and fifth choice, and so on, when it came to eating. To you it may sound unbelievable but it is true and after reading the diary excerpts below I feel sure you will agree.

March 3, 1945. We still have spuds and bread. Ran out of fuel today, so no heat.

March 4, 1945. Haircut. Boy that's great. Cold.....room. Made scavenger hunt of incinerators and sump to secure fuel. Got two paper boxes and 3 ½ logs (from sump). Things are really getting rough. Very little left to eat. Church sermon on three temptations of Christ. Good. Met Randolph Lee (went down in Jan. in a P-47 in the Brenner Pass). Also saw Burhmann again. Enjoy visiting with him. News today excellent. Canadians and Americans linked up north of Düsseldorf. Germans cracking in East Pomerania. Now I know first hand what it feels like to live in slums or back alleys and grub for a living in other people's garbage cans for a bare existence. I wonder just how long this can go on. Let's hope the war ends soon, so we get out of here with at least a little health and some flesh on our bones. Boy, I would gladly eat what "Ma" feeds the dogs now.

Some of the statements in the above entry will need clarification so before quoting more I shall proceed to do just that. The haircut mentioned was given to me by one of my roommates, with the shears and clippers that had been sent in by the YMCA. In our compound we had two such sets, and they had to make the rounds before another haircut was in order. By the time they had been to all the barracks at least two months would pass, after which we would receive the equipment again. Our hair would be long by that time in spite of how short it had been cut previously, unless we had it trimmed with the usual room equipment. This consisted of laying a sharp razor blade on the teeth of a comb and then combing as you ordinarily would. It at least helped immeasurably in keeping the hair out of our necks, and from running over our ears, which would otherwise have been the case. As for how the top looked that was not too important for no one would see us anyway except our buddies and they too looked just as we did, so would have no room for criticism. Randolph Lee was a fellow that I had gone through Jefferson barracks with, and now was meeting again for the first time. You could never be sure just who you would meet in prison camp next. March 5, 1945. I received my first letter and it was from my home church pastor. It contained the Christmas message, along with a Christmas card.

March 6, 1945. Food shortage is getting more acute by the day. Please God lets bring this horrible war to an end so we don't starve to death, for we've waited patiently all these months to get back home.

March 7. Rutabaga in today, so we have something besides potatoes and bread, which we had none too much of. Two letters from the folks (the first ones and Boy, was I glad to get them)!

Those two letters I received from home were surely welcome. This was the moment that I had been awaiting for many months. Now at least I knew they were all right as of the 11th and 17th of December, and that they were preparing for the Christmas season as always making the best of a bad situation, which I have every reason to believe for them was much more depressing and sad than it was for me. They could not be the least bit certain what was happening to me, while I could comfort myself with the fact that at least they were in reach of most anything they might need. Neither letter gave any indication that they had been receiving any of my letters, so I still did not know whether the letters that I had been writing were arriving or not.

March 8, 1945. (Notice on bulletin board). German rations per week are as follows:

```
Meat  . . . . . . . . . . . . . . . . . . . . . . . .4 oz.
Bread . . . . . . . . . . . . . . . . . . . . . . .1 loaf
Margarine  . . . . . . . . . . . . . . . . . . .4 ½ oz.
Dried Vegetables . . . . . . . . . . . . . . .4 ½ oz.
Barley  . . . . . . . . . . . . . . . . . . . . . .1 1/3 oz.
Cheese . . . . . . . . . . . . . . . . . . . . . .2/3 oz.
Sugar . . . . . . . . . . . . . . . . . . . . . . . .4 ½ oz.
Soup mix . . . . . . . . . . . . . . . . . . . . .1 ½ oz.
Potatoes . . . . . . . . . . . . . . . . . . . . . .7 lbs.
(never received even half of this)
Coffee  . . . . . . . . . . . . . . . . . . . . . . .1 oz. (ersatz)
```

Yes, you would really get fat on that, if you were a midget and ate but once every other day. Our camp doctors said this diet supplied us with 1100 calories a day, and also told us that the normal body required nearly 1300 just to lie in bed and hold its own, so you can readily imagine what happened to our bodies. In case you can not I might say that in March I weighed about 110 lbs., and when I entered the camp I weighed 168 pounds. Not bad, but it might have been better.

March 9, 1945. Volkstrum being checked out as "counters" for roll call. Soon all the old guards will be gone. Kriege No. check. Allies crossed the Rhine (Wednesday I believe). Finished ruler today. Getting thinner daily. Belt has to be drawn up at least 4 inches to hold pants on what is now pretty much of a skeleton. Lights from 8 until 9 p.m.

You no doubt noticed in reading the last entry that I mentioned the Volkstrum. This organization was the people's army or civilian army and they were nearly all 60 or more years old. They wore their World War I uniforms and would take over, releasing the men who had been here to go to the fighting front. That in itself was very encouraging to us for we knew they must be running very short of men when they scraped that close in the "bottom of the barrel" for material. Then men who were guarding here were between 50 and 60 themselves and if they had to go, it surely would not be too long before the final curtain came crashing down, but much to my surprise that was not to happen for at least two months yet. How they held on that long I shall never guess, it must be that it takes time for armies such as the mighty ones we now had rolling east to travel the distance required, repair and rebuild bridges, thus bringing complete occupation and defeat about.

Further excerpts from my diary I do not believe necessary to convince you of what actually transpired, so shall cease with those quotes already given.

On March 11, death struck and we lost one of our members due to a blood disease commonly called "Leukocytosis." In spite of the valiant efforts made by our medics it was impossible to save him.

March 18, tragedy struck our camp like it never had before. The air raid sirens had blown, which meant everyone was to be in his barracks. One of the boys, who was in at the time it sounded, was not aware that there was an Alert on, so inadvertently stepped out of the door. What happened is now history. He was shot right through the head, and killed instantly. Another went out to give him aid and was shot through the chest. Two in a matter of minutes. Whether the latter died I am not sure. I know he was removed to the hospital, where a major operation was performed in his behalf, but what the eventual outcome was I am not able to say.

Shortly thereafter we lost another man. This time it was from a cerebral hemorrhage that developed. The battle front news was good, but the camp situation was deplorable. Tragedy had struck and struck hard, leaving death and sorrow in its wake.

Now we thought the time had come for the guards to do a bit of worrying again for we had had more than our share of it in the past months, so via the reliable grapevine, all compounds were notified that at a specified hour on a certain day everyone should get out of the barracks and start to walk around the compound or gather into small mischievous looking groups on the playground. At the appointed hour everyone came out and started walking around the compounds. The grounds were a seething mass of humanity, nearly ten thousand men on the march, and gave our detainers plenty to worry about. They called out all the additional guards within the area armed them heavily and waited for results. They felt sure we were going somewhere, and from all indications one would be led to believe there was going to be a mass break. However, it was just a hoax to get the guards excited rather than let them go leisurely about their business. After all a little worry would do them good too, and at the same time provide us with a good laugh and a few happy moments.

So the month of March which was without a doubt the most severe starvation period we had gone through passed on, but before I leave it entirely I must tell you just one more incident that did happen, which I am sure you will find a bit difficult to believe, but it points out a very good lesson, namely, that as long as you have faith you will be fed, regardless of how it may come about. One night while a bitter cold windstorm was raging outside, along with a few snow flurries, a group of birds took it upon themselves to fly. While trying this feat, which is rarely done by birds at night, they became blinded due to the strong floodlights on the perimeter of the camp, and flew head on into the barracks and were killed. We heard various thumps on the building, but never once guessed what was actually occurring. We arose early the next morning went out and there much to our dismay lay the birds, dead and frozen. We gathered them up, took them to our respective rooms, dressed them and ate heartily that evening. Several of the boys were even fortunate enough to find ducks that had met with the same fate, however the majority of them were either starlings or sparrows. We were not particular just what they were, for food was food, regardless of what variety it might be. Yes, the hand of God must have been very close and was seeing to it that even though we were surrounded by barbwire on four sides and closely guarded, we would get something to eat. We were indeed very thankful for His blessings. I would say without fear of contradiction that the main reasons we were kept on such starvation rations during February and March were these: One Herr Hitler personally ordered all men executed at this camp who were in Air Corps and we all had been. Secondly the Germans themselves were looting the trains and warehouses that contained the Red Cross parcels, thus they never arrived. Even the guards at the camp looted our own warehouses so I surely would not put it above the ordinary civilians who now were feeling the pangs of hunger for the first time, to do likewise. We had very little to feast on in March but when April came along things changed drastically.

April the first, was Easter and one that I shall long remember. As we were walking out to roll call in the morning one of the boys in North I compound played Easter Parade on his trumpet. It was beautiful as it carried across the compound in the stiff south breeze that was blowing. The melody literally tugged at our heart strings and beckoned us back to the United States, but we must be patient and wait for the time had not yet arrived.

On April the third, who should walk into our camp, but one "Herr Max Schmeling." What a surprise! Here we had been laboring under the illusion that he was dead, but to our utter astonishment he was very much alive and well and to top things off, was a civilian. Well fed and fat, would be the best description I could give of him, other than the fact that he was very boastful, and nervy. He had brought autographed pictures with him and presented them to the prisoners who gathered around, but what happened to those same pictures would not be fit to tell. As for his boasts, well, the prime one was that once this war ended, and he doubted if that would take place for some time, he would beat us all back to the United States. How he had figured that out I do not know, nor for that matter am I in any position to say if it ever happened. Frankly I rather doubt if it did.

This month brought us everything good and we had few complaints to offer, for now for the first time in months we were getting a full Red Cross issue and the news was excellent. Every day it seemed to get better and we were busy indeed measuring distance, and keeping the score on how fast the Allies were approaching our camp. Each day the actual miles between us and our liberators was diminishing. We were really itching to get out and get started on that long trek back to civilization and home. How the Germans managed to get enough Red Cross parcels into the camp so that we could have one full parcel per man, per week, still remains a mystery. It seems to me that during the last month it would have been harder than at any other time during the war, for their transportation was almost at a standstill. It was being bombed and strafed incessantly all of which would lead me to conclude that nothing was moving. It is my honest opinion that they could quite easily have fed us as well during February and March if they desired, but somehow they saw fit to starve us off completely, which they nearly did. From the very day that I entered camp things kept getting worse and worse, and by the time the end of March had rolled around the handwriting on the wall was plainly evident, the only thing that staved it off was their change in policy.

Every day rumors would come into camp and be circulated by the rumor mongers that we were being evacuated. But where would they take us, or better said, where could they take us at this late stage for the Russians and the Americans were joining forces south of Berlin, unless they were going to take us by boat out to some of the small islands just off the peninsula and that did not seem too likely. There was only one other thing that they might do and that was to let Sweden come in and take us over there for she was a neutral. We were not supposed to be in a war zone according to the Geneva Convention, but I rather doubt if the Germans ever read that piece of paper more than likely they burnt it, just as they did all other treaties "Under the Linden" in Berlin.

The battle continued to rage, and when the 18th of April rolled around, Patton, the now famed third army General was 75 miles from the Russians and still going strong. Simpson, the 9th Army Chief, was but 88 miles from the Russians and closing in fast. The Russians were just a scant 95 miles from Stalag Luft 1, while the closest Americans were still 104 miles away. But both were inching their way steadily and April the 20th brought us the news we had been waiting anxiously to hear since the 31st of January. Namely that the Russians had laid down a tremendous artillery barrage and had now crossed the Oder River at Stettin and were again on the move. We had all heard the barrage, as we lay in bed, and could not help but wonder whether that was the one we had been anxiously awaiting. With the approach of nightfall confirmation had entered the camp. Now we were sure that was it.

We were almost beside ourselves in eager anticipation of the final day of liberation. Every hour that went by the gun fire drew closer and closer and so the gap between prisoners and liberators drew slowly shut. The Germans, so the grapevine reported, were moving all the civilians out of the area between Stettin and Stralsund, which meant that the Russians must be heading in this direction for Stralsund was but 18 miles away. What a lovely thought to harbor. News as to how close the troops actually were getting to the camp itself was very hard to get for none of the guards would talk on the subject, however, they readily admitted that the battle was raging in Berlin, further that it had been completely surrounded and that the Russians had joined forces with the Americans on the Elbe River. Our evacuation route was not cut, so there need be no additional worry about moving anymore. That rumor could be chucked into the ash can along with all the rest of the worthless surmises that were busy making people unhappy.

On the 27th of April we received word that the Russians were 83 miles from Barth and going strong. The following day news came in that they had cut the distance to 69 miles. We jumped and danced with glee for our liberators were definitely on their way. Each day they drew closer and on the 30th the Germans frankly told us the Russians were but 20 miles away. At this time they gave us permission to dig trenches in which we might seek cover should they decided to fight for this camp. Rumors were flying thick and fast that they were moving S.S. troops in to replace the Volkstrum and were going to fight it out with the Russians right here on this site. Could it be that we were to find ourselves directly in the center of a battle to the death on this the eve of liberation? We hoped not, but had no way of knowing, so everyone got busy and commenced digging.

What to dig with was the first problem, and we did not have very long to ponder over the situation either. It demanded immediate action or it would be too late for we could hear the "booming of guns" on the southern horizon already. That section of pipe we had removed when putting up the oven seemed the most logical solution for it was quite heavy gauge and thus could stand the digging strain. I slit it down the side with the table knife and the crude hammer we had, then opened it at the seam. This done, I had two pieces and so bent both of them into shape for the digging that was to begin. Thus the segment of stove pipe that had been useless for so many months had again come into its own and was doing a great job in a new field, namely removing dirt for the protection of our very lives. Other crude instruments used included tin cans, boards, and even the table knives themselves. Any way to get it removed, regardless of how prehistoric the method might have been. We worked feverishly and with all the zest at one command and by mid afternoon we had a zig zag trench completed that would accommodate everyone in the room and also had a trap door made in the floor of the room so that we might raise it up, jump into the passageway, and get out to the trench itself. The passageway we deemed a necessity for should they arrive unexpectedly it would provide us with a means of getting to the trench without ever so much as exposing ourselves to the gunfire that would undoubtedly be taking place. The trench had been well banked up and covered with sod, so would, we felt, be adequate protection from rifle and small arms fire. If anything bigger was used, we would have to trust to luck, for we had done everything possible. Up until this time we had had no place to hide or seek refuge during air raids or anything else, but had been living targets for anyone who saw fit to destroy us. The trenches at least gave us a feeling of security such as we had never experienced before.

But April the 30th had even more significance than that already mentioned. Col. Spicer, our former C.O. who had been sentenced to death was released from solitary confinement and brought back to our compound. Everyone yelled and cheered as he was brought in through the gates and once more permitted to take up residence with us. He had been spared, as we fervently prayed he would be, by a turn of events in the war. The fate of the Germans was sealed, and they knew it, so to carry out the unjust sentence they had pronounced would have served only to heap more scorn and hate on them than was already the case. We were very happy that they had made such a decision, even though we knew it was the turn of events that brought it about. Throughout the entire day they were busy blowing up their equipment in the large radar school which was just 1000 feet from our South compound. All during the war it had sat there in perfect peace and contentment, with never a worry, for to bomb it would have brought disastrous results to the prisoners. A beautiful location and I doubt very seriously whether it just happened to be there. The Germans are much smarter than we give them credit for. More than likely it had been planned that way. They knew full well that the allies would value the thousands of prisoners held here more than they did that school. Oh, how right they were!

At the close of the day 23:30 (11:30 P.M.) to be more specific, the Germans packed up lock stock and barrel and vanished into thin air leaving us in sole possession of the camp. I believe that they must have been afraid of being captured by the Russians so made their way to the American lines to give themselves up. At any rate the camp was now ours and so the Allied Commanding Officer stationed M.P.'s, who had been selected some time ago, in the guard towers and around the fences so the men would not venture out and thus get themselves killed by the Russians when they came in. We were free men, but would have to wait until it was safe, before going any distance from the camp. Very few of us could speak Russian, so would be unable to talk to them should we meet, and tell them who we were. Then too they had given ample warning that they would shoot anything that was moving, so it was best to "stay put" until they finally arrived. We did not have to wait long for the following day or May 1, 1945, at 22:30 (10:30 P.M.) the Russians arrived. When the first car drove up to the camp, everyone ran from the barracks, yelled and screamed to the top of his voice and really made merry, for now we were really free again, and in the hands of friendly allies. The air was wonderfully fresh and clean and to think that we need no longer stay in those barbed wire stockades, was almost more than we could believe ourselves.

So actually only 23 hours elapsed between the time the Germans left and the Russians entered, and during that time we had not sat idly by, twiddling our thumbs. Aside from taking over the entire camp and its operation, plus the radar school, a special detachment had been sent down to take over the Air Field at Barth, which they did, with no trouble. We who had been prisoners were now again busy fighting for the allies, helping them to take over all of Germany. Upon the arrival of the Russians the majority of the Americans, British and Canadians, who had been at this airport, came back to camp so as not to hinder Russians' mopping up operation. Also we wanted to participate in tearing down the fences, guard towers and everything else that we had grown to hate intensely.

The Russians were extremely generous and supplied us with all the food that they could find in the area. They went to Barth and got all the flour, bread and other edibles from the bakeries and shops and delivered them to the camp. They also drove into the confines of the camp a hundred head of milk cows, which they had taken from nearby farms. These served a dual purpose, for we milked some and butchered others. We had steak in unlimited quantities from the day of their arrival until we finally departed.

The second day they drove in another hundred head to supplement the first consignment, and now we were more than adequately supplied. Besides this they made available to us some 3000 head of hogs which they had at Barth, however, due to the large amount of steak on the hoof we never even bothered to butcher one. The cattle were butchered as needed by men within the confines of the camp and then the meat was cut up and delivered to the various rooms. Nobody was in want, all had more than they could eat for the first time since their arrival here. Naturally we could not eat much for our stomachs had shrunk to next to nothing, and so after eating one hamburger or piece of steak or at most two, they would be full. But that did not deter us, for we would just go out, lie down in the sun for awhile, then come in and eat again. Not once, not twice, but a dozen times a day if we were so inclined. There was no limit, the lid was off, so we ate until we nearly burst.

On May the 7th the Russians put on a show for us, comparable to those put on by the USO for our front line troops. The affair lasted four hours and consisted of dancing, acrobatics, singing, both choral and solos, and the orchestra. It was very entertaining and upon completion rather made me want to take a trip to Moscow for if those girls in that show were any indication of what might be found in Moscow it would not be a bad place to go. As a matter of fact would prove very enjoyable. It might have been because I had not seen women for such a long period that they impressed me so, but it goes without saying that at the time they were very nice looking and made a very good impression on all of us. The entire cast was very friendly and highly pleased with the appreciation we had shown them in the form of applause for their show, which was all in Russian dialect, and thus not understandable to many of us. We did however have an American interpreter on the stage explaining some of the things as they went on and that helped considerably.

When the show had been completed I went back to the barracks and there found they were passing out the interrogation records that had been taken from the German files. I was certainly happy that they had not had the time to destroy them, before leaving, for this gave me the opportunity of seeing just what the interrogator had written under comments. In German it stated "A very good soldier," which from any enemy officer is indeed a compliment. This rating comes only to those who refuse to talk and show good military bearing, for they realize full well that good soldiers follow both principles to the letter. I have been told that allied interrogators use the same quotation, when they run into a German who refuses to talk, so I assume both allies and Nazis must have the same feeling in regard to those principles when it comes to dealing with captured military personnel. Military discipline indicates to them that you are a well-trained soldier.

Every day that passed brought us renewed hopes that soon the evacuation of the camp would begin, but while we were still here we made the best of the time. We were free to go fishing in the Baltic, or do most anything we liked on the Peninsula on which we found ourselves until finally moved out, even to the extent of hunting some of "Herr Goerring's" prized deer. I am very happy to say that some of those prized possessions disappeared "via the frying pan" during our waiting period too. I doubt whether he ever missed them for chances are, he would never get back to look after his former interests anyway. Many of us built rafts, and thus fetched boats the Germans had tied up out in the deep water. Once we had them we would either go sailing or just plain boating on the placid waters of this renowned sea. It was a great sport many of us had heretofore never enjoyed in our lives, so we took every advantage of it.

May the 12th, evacuation began on a small scale and during the day nearly 900 prisoners were flown out in B-17's from the Barth Air Field. By nightfall they had worked out all the plans for the following day's operating and promptly at 12:30 on the 13th day of May, I was on my way in a "winged steed" to France. It had taken me a long time to finish my last mission and fly back but now I was making the grade.

At Camp Lucky Strike, St. Valery, France, we received from the Government a complete issue of clothes, as a replacement for those we had been wearing when shot down. There were 70,000 or more of us in that camp at the time so you can see what a job it was. Besides this we were given a kit containing the necessary toilet articles. This was a gift of that never forgetting life sustaining American Red Cross and contained this message.

"On behalf of the people of the United States of America, the American Red Cross extends warm greetings to liberated American prisoners of war. In the name of your loved ones at home we salute you for your sacrifices for them and your Country..." It was encouraging to know that at least someone appreciated what we had gone through. The gift was deeply appreciated.

I stayed at Camp Lucky Strike for one month, questioning everyone I saw regarding the fate of my still missing crew members. Then I flew back to my old base in England to turn in the report on what I knew had happened to them. While at the base I also checked all the reports they had on the flight, and found that Sgt. Damrel, the engineer who had bailed out and had never been seen again, was repatriated. Why, I had no way of knowing, so for that information I would have to wait until I got back to the States and could see him personally. I also secured all the information I could regarding our personal belongings which supposedly had been gathered up by the squadron and sent back to Kansas City, Missouri. As a final move I secured the names of the next of kin of all the boys on our crew, so that I might contact them personally upon arrival in the States and give them the information to which they were rightly entitled. I arrived in the States June 30, or two months after liberation, but it was well into the month of October before I had finished seeing the parents, wives, brothers and sisters of the men concerned. Try as I might to accomplish it sooner, it proved impossible for I was still in the army and so had duties to perform. Whenever I had several days off I would contact the nearest commercial airline, explain to them why I wanted space, and where I wanted to go. I never waited more than four hours to get underway, so grand was their cooperation. I tried to get a priority but was told it was impossible to get one for such purposes, so traveled, "catch as catch can." Through the splendid efforts of the airlines, a truly difficult job was finally completed. To them, and to the next of kin, concerned, I owe everything.

To the American Red Cross, I owe my life, health and actual being, for without their timely supplies of food sent into prison camp, neither I nor anyone else in that camp would have been alive today to tell the story.

To the YMCA, I owe more thanks than can ever be given for their grand efforts in supplying me and thousands of other fellows, with some small measure of entertainment. Without it, many more men would have gone totally insane than was now the case. And last, but by no means least, goes the thanks, praise and eternal gratitude of the thousands in prison camp, to the Almighty, ever Merciful GOD, who never forgot but led us safely through the escapade. To Him, and to all of the aforementioned, I owe the opportunity of writing this book. Without anyone of them, it would have been virtually impossible.

"FINIS"